THE TEACHINGS OF THE OCEAN

by Jernej Rakušček

D1728641

Ljubljana, 2016

Published by Jernej Rakuscek, 2016

Layout and Cover Design/Photo by Jaka Adamic (www.adamic.com.au)

Published in Slovenia in 2016 (2nd Edition)

Printed and bound in Slovenia by Tiskarna DEMAT

ISBN: 978-0-646-57317-5

National Library of Australia Cataloguing-in-Publication entry

Author: Rakuscek, Jernej.

Title: The teachings of the ocean / Jernej Rakuscek.

ISBN: 9780646573175 (pbk.)

Subjects: Life skills.
Surfing.
Water.

Dewey Number: 646.7

To my brother, Andraž,
who has introduced me to surfing,
and so changed my life
and the life of many.

Mahalo.

Who has the
final say?
... Period

Aloha
&
Mahalo
&

TABLE OF CONTENTS

There is someone who has the power
to change the world at once. You.

FOREWORD

Jernej Rakušček, the author of this book, is a creative visionary. His demeanour is centered, balanced, and spiritual. Wherever he goes or whatever he does, he is at peace with himself and his surroundings. A multi-talented athlete whose purpose is to extend his knowledge and teachings, he hopes to improve the quality of your world and share his experiences to enlighten you, inspire you, and set you in motion to achieve your dreams and goals.

Realistically, Jernej's life appears to be a night of unexplainable dreams, some good and some bad. However, these dreams are real and he goes the full distance to accomplish and live them. His approach to life has enabled him to take advantage of opportunities as a means to enrich his life and create purpose and meaning for others.

Mr. Zen's, as many view him, connectedness with nature and the ocean is the force behind his humble and respectful demeanour. He understands the importance of how his spiritual awareness has enabled magnificent moments to enter his life without trying to question his actions or decisions. The result is greater learning, higher awareness, deeper respect, and less ego.

These attributes he has mastered and is a role model as a peaceful warrior which will enable him to continue his journey as one of the least known, bravest, courageous, calm big-wave riders I have ever seen.

Don, Hawai'i, July 2010

We shall start our journey at the beginning. This might be even later in the past than you think. It is before you were born. It is actually happening to someone who is yet to become someone. This means it might be your past, but it is someone's present. So, we will stay in the present.It begins with the water environment of your mother's womb. It is dark. It is wet. It is usually a quiet, safe place. A place to grow and expand. You rely completely on the flow of nutrients from your mother to your body through a small tube. You are connected.

For the time being, the time of body expansion has gone by and it is time to leave this place. Going into the unknown. Towards the bright light. Again.

As air enters the body, you feel a never-felt-before sensation of expanding lungs and the whole chest area. Breath jumps in and connects you to this world. Crying is understood. It is about leaving an old, well-known, safe haven and coming into a complete unknown. Not to mention too much about the fact that most of the water environment is gone. But you will be bathing in a bath tub or a pond soon enough...

TO LEAD INTO

This is a book about water. A book about energy. It is a book about life. About a human life. About how a human life can be humane. For oneself and for others. It is a book about a journey of a wave. It is a book about surfing and about how you can develop skills to enjoy every moment of the ride.

The contents that intertwine through this book have been observed, examined, used and experienced over five years of living next to the ocean around the world. I write about one ocean, since in my opinion there is only one body of water on planet Earth. One ocean.

The actual words of the book have been written in one flow of consciousness; after years of putting pieces together, I grabbed a pen and wrote from start to finish in fluidity, without major corrections, additions or abstractions. The book had been written between November and February 2009/2010 in Hawaii. I went there to get the final insights for it. Seeing how the contents, which I wished to describe, were manifesting themselves over the days showed me what it was to be done. In that sense, the story is also some kind of a diary, where experiences of the ocean, water, energy, human life and surfing flow from one to another, one into the other. Names of most people in the book have been altered. All events happened in reality.

After deeply experiencing many recreational activities, surfing has proven to be the only one that is not only the most fun, the most enjoyable to me, but also the one where wisdom of energy, water, mind, body and the universal spirit is so plainly at work. That's why I wish to share this wisdom through showing you the similarities of surfing and a human life on land. Showing you how surfing can improve the quality of your being and giving you all the necessary tools to start learning this amazing art on the physical level. Hopefully inspiring you for something new and good. The rest is all yours.

We will go on a journey. We will take our body, our mind and go for a session. Surfing is like life. That is how we will share the lessons, which hold the potential to improve all aspects of your being. We will also learn basic surfing skills and how they directly relate to life skills on land.

Throughout 30 years of investigating mind and body, how they interact with the spirit in a process of learning a new movement, a unique method for learning and teaching surfing has been developed. In our journey through this book, though, we will address surfing as much as needed to inspire you for this art of motion.

Let us begin.

Our planet is blue. It is a planet of water. There is no life without water on this planet. A human body is more or less water.

Energy is never still. It is everywhere, yet in motion all the time. Changing. Adapting. Flowing in waves of endless possibilities, bending around optional outcomes and breaking into a single experience.

Chaos turns into order. Dots connect. A ride is born.

Life is movement.

A human life is a ride from one experience through the connected dots into the other one and back into the energy pool. From birth through the life's journey into death and back into the line-up to wait for another wave.

May you enjoy every single moment of your ride, which is you.

Aloha.

PROLOGUE

First check-in on a three-day journey to Hawaii.

I had a feeling that carrying two pieces of hand luggage onto a low cost carrier might be a problem. I still decided to take my guitar and the surfboards. Even though I am going to Hawaii as a surfer first, music is a huge part of my life.

The bag and the surfboard bag got checked in easy, weighing just right. Seems like I developed rare traveller's skills to pack according to airline baggage rules.

"So, I have this small backpack as a carry on and this small guitar. Will that be OK?"

"Huh. No. You can only carry one item on board."

"It says in the policy (which I read every time) that a musical instrument can be carried on board, if it's small." (It is a mini guitar indeed.)

"That's right sir, but you can carry on board one item."

"What if I then checked it in and pay an extra item. How much? 22 Euros? That would go."

"You would also then have an excess overall baggage weight. We would have to charge you 22, plus 10 Euros per kilo. Your guitar bag looks really soft and that might be another problem."

"What if I just tried it? You think the staff in the boarding area would say something."

"The two of us are that staff. And, hm, yes, we would say a thing."

Slovenia is really small. What then? OK. I am going to Hawaii and it is time to learn ukulele. Fine. The guitar stays here. No problem.

No problem? There was no problem in reality. You see, as I was sitting on the plane and waited for the take-off, it occurred to me. I could have taken things from the backpack and simply pack the guitar bag with them. The mini guitar and a proper guitar size bag were a perfect match. It got me thinking.

Some people say there is no problem that does not have a solution. That is true. Any way things go wrong, they can be undone. Some people focus on the problem. It just makes it bigger. Some people ignore the problem. It just gets worse and causes more responses. Wiser people focus on solutions and solve problems really fast.

I began thinking that the SOLUTION is what causes the problem. That the problem appears, so the solution could be found. Going back in time. Think about it with the guitar case.

There was already a way for me to take everything. The guitar, boards, laptop, camera, and all that stuff in the backpack. The solution was waiting for me. My last day was so intense with keeping up. I did not even take time to ponder solutions about the guitar. The problem appeared and I failed to see to which solution it pointed to.

Do it. Next time when something you see as a problem comes along, simply ask:

What SOLUTION is this problem guiding me to?

After all, life is not complicated if we do not make it complicated. Ask Mother Nature. No problems there...

THE TEACHINGS OF THE OCEAN

DETERMINATION

We go from no will and all choices
to all will and no choices,
until we decide to create.

Saturday night. The full moon was full two nights ago. This is usually the time when I don't consciously sleep. Even when I lay, I stay awake. The dreaming world might be around me, but I know I am sleeping, so I keep awake. Sometimes things keep on rolling late into the night. This was one of them.

Checked out the swell forecasts for Hawaii and how they affected "the Eddie". Eddie Aikau was one of the most famous humans to embody the aloha spirit. His life and love for the ocean were blended into one. His ways of living on land were inspired extensions of lessons in the ocean. Humble. Fluid. Adaptable. Determined. Without a projected self.

That's how he knew what would happen. He felt the ocean and took along the surfboard on the sailing journey. What a life! A few days later, it hit me. What kind of feelings must have he been going through before leaving?

To honour his life and the early death, the Hawaiian community, in collaboration with world's leading surf industry manufacturers, created a prestige big wave contest. One for which entry on the basis of money or ratings points is disregarded. You need to be invited. A true honour to surf Waimea Bay in an event like this. To further pay respect to Eddie, who was known to surf "The Bay" when it was big, a limitation to wave heights has been added. The waves have to be at least 20 feet tall on the face.

This swell was right. The call has been made. Monday, Tuesday, Wednesday. I booked the flight on Monday noon. This is where I started to do a living experiment. One that is going on at this very moment. How to fully trust and be guided by the aloha spirit. The essence of life. Connectedness to the source through water.

There was a little something I decided to do on the morning of my flight from Maui to Oahu. The aloha told me I had time. Wind affecting the sea and producing too unsettled conditions. This, among other things to follow, turned out to be a true foresight later on.

What does it mean to trust yourself? Which part exactly of who you think you are that relates to? Is it your mind? Your heart? A thought or a feeling?

It is definitively something that has power and direction to guide on the way to happiness. Not to happiness, but to create a way where happiness is an ever-lasting companion.

I did not trust myself. For that, no one is to blame. Not my friends, nor myself. Forgiveness produces wisdom out of "mistakes". Obviously, the Australian driver's license was not enough to get me on the plane. Thank you, Val, for your pick-up.

Time moves differently in Hawaii. When you let go here, things seem to fall into places just right. So, I played guitar, while dear friends Nicole and Val got ready for their mini surf trip and the evening party at Honolua Bay. Twenty minutes to the plane. Boarded in time. Why did I have to go back for my passport?

Simple. To call Waimea Backpacker's, book a bed and create an opportunity to later ride some big waves at "The Bay".

I got to the hostel at night. Walking up to hut number seven, I saw a big wave board, called a gun, laying on the lawn up front. Waimea was calling. Brandon had surfed it a couple of times. He advised I get a big, big board.

Next day, "the Eddie", after five years of no go, happened. It has been 31 years from Eddie's death. I have 31 years in this body. Watching "the competitors" take on the live ocean and the energy travelling through, I fell into a trance. I travelled back in time to my birth year – 1978.

I knew I was the only one capable of paddling to shore and get help. It was not my strength or boldness or courage. None of these. We all simply knew, rationally through the memory of the events and irrationally by feeling the wisdom in the moment that no one else of the capsized boat had the connection to the ocean I had. The captain was an honest and a fair man. Responsible. He tried to persuade me not to go. In the end, he knew it was the only way. Eddie had to go.

Waimea was breaking at twenty to thirty feet wave face heights that day. No clouds in the sky. Perfect breeze. The sun started blazing around 1 pm. I started thinking about the trance. About Eddie. About the connection to water and energy I have. About how surfing and the ocean affect my life. About how they affected Eddie's with an ultimatum. Imagine. Imagine, something you loved or held such an intimate relationship with would eventually be the place of your death. Even more. The place of dying. A process, not a single momentary event.

They never found Eddie's body. With respect, I could only feel why.

Seeing my homeland drift sideways of my view, it became clear to me. The current is too strong and I am too weak. No sense in fighting the current. The ocean is greater than I am. Just rest on the board. Flowing back to the source. It has been hours. Hunger, dehydration, soreness. Pain. Then, suddenly, no more pain. Still alive. No more I. Just the ocean. Thank you, Eternal Sea. Mahalo Kai Noa. Time to leave this vessel here and return to the homeport.

What a story! What a man. I need to honour him and surf Waimea within this swell. Where could I find a proper gun within what is left of the afternoon?

Coming back to the backpacker's from Haleiwa, I was smiling inside. I had bought a ten foot leash, wax and a wetsuit top. I also had two phone numbers of local people who would help me find a proper board for tomorrow. Surely enough, they did not pick up or return my calls the same evening. The voice said again: "Just trust the Aloha spirit."

What do you do when you cannot see what else you could do?

You trust, believe or pray. I decided to follow the trust in aloha. It has so far guided and supported my teaching and travelling around the world. Always keeping me in touch with the ocean. Source of all life. So, I went to bed with ease.

Local roosters and chickens announced a new day. There was a familiar feeling – Waimea is still breaking. The swell is still big enough. With stillness, I went for a walk, exercised on the cliff and observed the breaking waves. The small figures taking six meter drops. Trusting and believing started to look different. An hour later I joined them in the ocean on a brand new, at least for me, ten feet gun.

Normally, it was time for breakfast. Morning exercise done, the waves checked. So far, so good.

I was wondering at how calm I was in spite of not having a board to surf those waves. Then, a man walks straight to our porch and asks for Brandon.

"I think, he is still sleeping." I said. He lingered. "There probably wouldn't be any harm if you go in and wake him up." I encouraged. He did. They were out on the lawn in a few minutes. Talking surf. How amazing the sessions they had at Waimea were. How it was out there this morning. How getting back to his place with such a big board is a hassle.

"Especially, since I am leaving today." The man said.

"I might be able to help you with that." I offered.

We agreed on the price and off we were. Jeremy and Jernej on their journeys. Thank you. Aloha.

Paint a picture. With your mind. Put yourself into a situation where you have no control. The only power you have is how to adapt to what you observe is happening. Observing, learning and choosing are your tools. The environment is moving all the time. No pause. No break. Constant fluid motion. Your efforts are focused to find order in chaos. Realize the potential that you already see. Create a ride. Experience the joy of being connected. Gliding effortlessly. Yet, no two waves break the same. The concept can be grasped, but it also needs to be let go in every moment. Fixation in the ocean creates conflicts.

There he was. A man born in a waveless country.

No surf culture or surf awareness whatsoever. He stood up on the board for the first time at the age of twenty. To his current age of 31, he has had five years of surf experience. There he was. Sitting amongst the same, but completely different people. The ocean that day offered him thirteen rides on five to six meter waves. He received them with humbleness and gratitude.

Trusting in aloha spirit has no more seemed as a theoretical or purely mental exercise. It produces straightforward material events with ease and fluidity. I started to realize how my view of surfing through life had been correct. It started opening up to me that it was indeed possible to experience every day on land as a direct metaphor of a surf session in the ocean. That it was possible to use the same approach of acting in the ocean for deciding and acting in everyday situations. The feeling of this reality had been there for a long time. But this time, in Hawaii, it has begun to become an aware transition. Do you understand?

It means to take lessons from an activity and use them in everyday decision making, choice choosing, possibility creation and practical experiencing. Seeing that they, lessons and ways of attitude, produce a lifestyle full of presence, happiness and effortless acting, still seems incomprehensible. This book, though, shows the logic behind it all. Surfing is more than an art, sport or leisure activity. It is a re-creation, for when we fully do it, we recreate our being. Time and again.

A Hawaiian shaman explained the true meaning behind the word Aloha. Yes, it is widely used today for expressing "thank you", "you're welcome", "see you soon", "nice to meet you" or "welcome" and for similar social interactions of kindness and gratitude. Since there is a bridge between relating a word so unique into another cultural environment of another group, a longer translation was needed. The shaman spoke: "When we say Aloha, we are basically expressing that (I) joyfully share (my) life's energy with you in this moment."

That means aloha spirit is a spirit, which recognizes life's energy, this moment and sharing it all with others in the ambience of love.

Hut number seven. Top bed on a bunk. Straight in front of "my" bed, what can I see? A wooden carving with one word written: Aloha.

What does it mean to trust aloha?

It means to be focused on staying in the present and doing actions where one feels joy when relating to another being: object, plant, animal and/or human.

The swell has diminished in size overnight. Waimea is no longer breaking. The obvious choice was to go and watch the best professional surfers in competition. Their world tour finishes in Hawaii at one of the most technical, and deadliest, waves on the planet. It is named Banzai Pipeline.

The human race, which seems to be racing somewhere, has the tendency to name things. Whether for communicational purposes, data memory or possession inclination, it is still good to remember that a name is only a name. It is not the essence of a being to which it has been given. A surf spot, as in the place where waves for surfing occur, can be named. A wave, on the other hand, is a passing phenomenon. It is good to remember this, because it gives the freedom to come back to the present moment and simply observe what is there, without any predetermined conceptions of fear, courage, self-projections or similar.

This view comes into play on land when coming to "known" places, meeting "famous" people, interacting with "powerful" individuals or simply communicating with someone, about whom you have heard this and that. Get it? Just be, observe and act accordingly by trusting aloha.

When we have a wish, what is in our power to actually do in order for that wish to come true? Is it just wishing and than sitting on the porch in front of a backpackers hut, waiting for the wish to get manifested? It does not seem like it.

"What is in my power to find two good boards as soon as possible?" I asked myself on the morning of the Pipeline competition. Not that I was competing, but I did wish to surf as soon as possible. A competition of my own.

I believe that whatever idea for the next step

seems/feels the best at that moment, say in a project we pursue, is the fastest way towards realizing a wish come true.

I decided to make a sign and display it on the beach while watching competition. Funny enough, the girl, who played a crucial role in getting the magical board, sat down right next to me and did not see the sign in the first place.

The wave comes to you. You need to know where to wait for it. Follow aloha. As Duke Kahanamoku once said: "There is always a wave behind." Sure, no two waves are the same. You get one chance to ride that wave. But you always get a chance for another ride. Always. That, to me, is a soothing realization.

we always meet for a reason
that reason is you
that reason is me
you have come across my path, so I could give you
something no one else could ever give you
so, baby, please call me or send me a txt

the reason why I'd like to see you tonight
is so that I could give you the light
that you've been after for so long
people misguide you, so you'd come along

I don't have time to give you everything you're after
But I do have time to show you how you could have
everything you already possess

Mr. Sunnyfunny and Mrs. Sunshine are walking down
the street
Their stepping rhythm is making people move their
dancing feet

May you be happy
May you find your freedom
May you keep smiling
May you find your way home

If you ever wish to find me,
I'll be right here, right now.
If you ever wish to touch me,
Darling, we are already in touch.

After all, we all carry around the same, same seed.
After all, we are all swimming in the same, same sea.

GENEROSITY

Whatever is worth having, is worth sharing.

I was having a conversation with George on my left, while we enjoyed watching some of the best athletes surf Hawaiian waves. Meanwhile, Lisa on my right, on her phone and suddenly she passed it on to me and said:

"My friend Don might sell you a 6'8". He really isn't trying to sell it, because it's a special board, but maybe you would take a look at it and like it. Here, you can just talk to him..."

It was funny. As they say in USA: hilarious. I was giving my card to George and writing down my phone number and talking to him, while Lisa extended her hand and waited for me to take the phone and talk to her friend.

"Just give me a moment, Lisa. Let me give George my contacts and explain what kind of boards I am looking for."

Back in the office. In a few moments, I found myself enchanted by this man's voice and his description of a magical board he has.

"You'll see, man. It's a very special board. I'm not kidding! I don't really wish to sell it, but you can have a look at it...Well, the leash plug broke and it was a sign for me not to ride it again... It's almost brand new...They don't make boards like that anymore... I don't know man... Maybe $250... Yes, call me up in the evening and we can meet... Oh, really? I live ten minutes away from where you are... Ok, so we'll talk later. Aloha."

Our later evening phone conversation brought up an issue of value. Such a special board, he said, he could not sell it for less than $330. Interesting, I thought, how many times did I see the value of an item go up during the bargaining?

Sure, the owner usually has a high price. The buyer offers a lower one and the game starts. This one felt completely different. I was interested to find out more about this board. I could not afford $330, so I did not have any feelings of obligation. In a day's time, I bought it for $400 and paid $40 for the leash plug repair. Here's why:

"When Don crossed the parking lot with the board under his arm, I felt a sensation of lightness. This is exactly what I should be, and am, doing in this moment. This is the man I am suppose to meet and this is "the magical" board for me to surf these waves here."

The shape of the board, needless to add, was as I'd dreamt of. Now, the colours. The colours matched the colours of my t-shirt, shorts and the writing on the t-shirt.

You see, there are no coincidences as most people think of them. All things are happening at the same time. That is what the word means.

Co-incide. To happen together. Everything is connected. Everything is changing now. Together. At the same time.

Sometimes, though, so many things link together into a pattern that we recognize it. We say: "What a coincidence that A happened just when B was taking place." Signs? Definitely. For what? For us to recognize the path we choose to be on. Choose fully. This is how things start flowing from one into another without effort. Living in synchronicity. Some call it harmony.

When you have your eyes, spirit, ears, senses, mind, and intuition open to the information in the environment, you are in now, you fully recognize direction, what and how to do the next step. You choose. Life guides.

Our meeting regarding the board was extremely short. We could both immediately identify that the board waited for me for a long time. As my money matters stayed blurred, we could not discuss the price. One way or another aloha will help me to buy the board. Use it. Leave it in Don's careful, trustful hands, when I'm not in Hawaii.

Surfing saved his life. We didn't go into it. What is important is the realization you have for yourself. Surfing did not save my life. It gave me life. Not in a sense that I did not know before what I enjoy doing, what I wish to do professionally or that I had an existential crisis. You know, the whole "why I was born?" deal. Not at all.

It gave me life as it connected me to the ocean, outside and inside. Relax. Open your mind and read. There is always enough time to judge later on.

The human body is more or less an ocean. Seventy-five percent of the whole volume is represented by water. Inside the cell, there's even more of it. Ninety percent, give or take. Now, interestingly enough, the minerals that are in those two oceans, inside and outside of the cell, correspond to minerals found in the ocean/sea water. Chemically, as far as which and how many minerals are in it, the human blood resembles ocean salt water by ninety-five percent. When you are given a transfusion, it is basically (sea) salt liquid. What does it all mean?

WATER

May you be like water, baby.
May you flow into the ocean.
May you be like water.
Fluid in your motions.
Keeping your foolish notions.

May you be like water.
React simultaneously.
Adapt instantly.
Flow relentlessly.
Show so clearly.

May you feel like water.
Staying in your fluid emotions.
Flow around the rock, as if
the rock isn't there.
Feeling it dissolve away.

I won't worry.
No, I won't worry
about this rock.
I'll just flow around it.
Yet, I shall keep my will and direction.

May you be like clear crystal water.
May you see clearly.

Through it all, the lies and deceptions.
They want to create a world with no exceptions.
But who can overpower the nature?

If we are a part of this existence,
how could we control it?
And, this water planet of ours
is truly blue?

People absolutely love to argue and fight. It gives them a feeling of power. The struggle for power empowers some. The less inner power/strength someone has, the more of the external one she/he will seek. How to know the quantity of your inner power?

Simply rest in any position with you eyes closed and with no movements. How long can you last and stay peaceful?

We all know argue/fight/war is the opposite of peace. It is impossible to argue facts. Events exist with or without human awareness. Let us take gravity for example.

No matter, if we had grasped it intellectually or not, it would keep affecting. No matter what you call it. No matter, if you agree or disagree to it. Its fundamental principle stays the same all across existence: smaller is attracted by bigger. That's it. You wish to argue that? Come on, let us move on.

The same attitude goes for how the human body is composed. How it works. How the cell interacts with the environment. What it needs to fully function. What it does not need. Regardless of what you believe in, where you live, where you were born, what you do to survive. Of course, yes. You can argue/fight a fact. It will only create resistance, conflict and eventually bring you down. Like gravity. Why fight an ocean, when it is so much more powerful then you? Why not learn from it, adapt to it and use its endless energy to play, express, recreate and live?

Surfing gave me life, because it showed me how to take the lessons gained from interacting with energy and water, and live those attitudes on land. Of all human activities for "free" time, it is the only one, where the elements of nature come together in their pure form. Surfing came to people, not the other way around. Here's how it happens:

The sun (fire) heats up the atmosphere (air). Hot air rises and expands in an upward spiralling action. Unheated air flows in to fill space. The result is wind. The ocean (water) embraces the energy of that motion. It reacts to the wind and energy starts to travel across the ocean. When the wave energy comes across an obstacle, it bends around it. The ocean floor (earth) makes the wave break its journey and offers the experience of a ride. The human uses the board (originally wood) to glide with the wave until it finishes its long path. The energy of a broken wave moulds the earth, as it has done for ages (three quarters of this planet's surface is an ocean).

What I chose to do on the day of flying from Maui to Oahu, was to see a plastic surgeon. No, I am completely content with the external appearance of this body. It is the interior deformation, which I suffered while training a martial art of karate that has slowly, but surely, almost driven me to madness.

Almost ten years ago, a punch into my nose has

deformed the shape of the nostrils. The right one became extremely narrow, while the left one expanded significantly. As a result, both parts of the brain started being stimulated unproportionally. That has enabled me to venture deep into the intuitive world, as well as disabling me to use the analytical power of the mind to balance impulsive actions. A lot of bliss, insights and revelations. A lot of unnecessary suffering caused by irrational decisions when rational ones were called for. In the process I lost the partner for a lifetime. Do not even ask me about money matters.

Left and right nostril both stimulate one part of the brain. Since each part effects the opposite side of the body, the left nostril corresponds to the right side of the brain and vice versa. The left side of the brain has been determined to be in charge for analytical thinking, focus on details, where power for actions comes from and where the decisive centre to use logical arguments lies. Based on social conditioning of our society according to gender, we could call it "the male" side. To achieve balance, the right side of the brain, being activated with the flow of oxygen through the left nostril, is "feminine". It is a place, where feelings are reasons for decisions, where motivation for actions is born, where seeing how a detail fits in the whole picture is more crucial, and finally, where intuition dorms. We will not go into exactly what intuition is on this journey. There are so many ways for you to explore it.

The important thing here is to realize that any extreme causes imbalance and imbalance causes a lot of problems. Being extremely masculine is as dysfunctional as being extremely feminine. I am speaking on a psychological, mental level, not biological. Biologically, our gender is determined. However, our mind/spirit/soul/being does not have a gender. We face a challenge to balance both extremes and contribute to any relationship as a whole entity, capable of giving and receiving without the act of taking.

Eventually, we see something went far enough. On any level. We can then decide for action and boldly venture into change that will somehow create a better tomorrow. Or, we can choose inaction and remain frustrated. I usually tend to decide for action. So, I went to see one of renowned plastic surgeons in Hawaii, and USA for that matter, dr. Larry.

Upon examining me on the day of the big swell for Eddie and 68th anniversary of Pearl Harbour attack, he explained to me that the procedure is a simple one and also does not cost much. After telling me the price, I could see how much our value in money differed. He gave me a few minutes to think about it. He then told me a personal story. The story was a sign strong enough for me to say "yes" to the operation and pay quite a lumpy size of dollars from a travelling, life-sponsored budget.

He said that in his early days of surgery practice,

while still being fairly unknown and in a process of a fast learning curve, his father called him one day and said:

"I am looking at an excellent watch that you will buy."

Larry got surprised by the statement, but got intrigued with the decisive tone in his father's voice.

"Why would I want to buy a new watch? I have one and I like it."

"Trust me." Said the father. "You will buy this watch and it will do you a great service for you career."

"Ok." Larry gave in. "How much is it then?"

When the father told him, he got shocked.

"Why would I want to spend a ridiculously big amount of money for something I don't really need?" he protested.

"Just trust me, Larry." Father insisted.

After thinking about it for a while, Larry bought the watch. He had no idea why he was doing it, but he felt his father was right. He decided to trust.

Clients, who came in for their first informal meeting, often commented the great watch on his wrist. It is not hard to believe that it also gave them an impression of Larry's successful practice. Nowadays, he does not wear it anymore. As his skills and references excelled, there's no need for it anymore.

I also decided to trust. Here I am. Waiting for the

operation in the reception area. Remember? There are no coincidences. Everything is a co-incide-nce. There are signs to tell us if we are on the path we chose to be. If we are open to feel or/and see them.

Bus route 52 from Oahu's north shore to Honolulu is a long route. Yet, amazingly enough, it stops in front of the hostel (hut number seven) and runs to a part of the city, where it has a stop a couple of yards away from Larry's Oahu clinic and a stop a block away from the hospital where he will operate on me today. The operation room is on the 7th floor. Route 5+2=7.

I could go on, but I will not burden you at this point with more "hard2accept" theories. I sincerely urge you to try this attitude for a week. Be open to what the situation is telling or showing you. You have nothing to lose as you can return to the usual, the known attitude. On the other hand, you have a lot to gain.

I thanked Don for his time and told him that I will buy the board. When, I did not know. There were some things I needed to get sorted out beforehand. It has to feel right. Being a man of aloha spirit, he understood exactly what I meant.

Earlier this year I met a wealthy man. A self-made multimillionaire. A married man for forty years and a joyful marriage it appeared to be. They were sharing an income of a couple of hundred dollars and lived in a really, really small flat, shortly after meeting. He must have been doing some good financial reasoning, if he went from that to an estate as big as he owned it now. On his own, without family heritage. He was kind enough to share some of his mental guidelines with me. One of those was:

"Trying to make an investment and save up at the same time does not sound like a good idea."

So true. How could you achieve one goal, while focusing on actions of its exact opposite at the same time? You either invest and take the risk or you save up and wait.

That's why it dawned on me not only to buy Don's board, but also to up the price to $400 and then buy it. I would have to feel alright with the price, since I am making an investment. An investment in happiness can never be a bad one.

In one way or another, tomorrow is a creation of today and today somehow bears the fruit of yesterday. Investing your money and/or energy into what fills fully your being can only lead to attract more of the same quality in your life. And you are guided as we speak.

The place of my operation was close to "The Board of Water Supply". Life has an amazingly witty sense of humour if you can see it. Think about it. My life as a Slovenian, waves, water, how surfing brought me to Hawaii and the photo on page 140.

Monica, Larry's secretary, took me to her home, where I spent the night after the operation, just in case I would need someone. Her home address number was 4003. Harry turned sixty-eight just weeks ago. 6+8=14, which can be two times seven. Yes, or a five. That's my point.

We choose the signs accordingly to our focus on the life's path. You can do and be anything and anyone you choose to do and be. You are already doing and being it.

On another note, I really do not have any desire whatsoever to go into any Western medicine hospital on behalf of any health issues ever again in this lifetime. They are, in spite of all the warmth of people who work there, a cold and lonely place where the human mind assumes the disposition of god over the human body, and moreover the essence of its being. You really do not have any assurance that you will be healed. Cured yes, healed no. It is supposed to be understood. Still, how many people do you know that the hospital really, once and for all, healed?

That is right. The strongest domain of any Western medicine hospital is a procedure where raw, fast changes of body's functions take place – an operation. For that, may all concerned be blessed. Not only for the return of my whole breath, but also for all those walking with healed legs and reincarnated souls with new hearts. Seriously. Technologically, Western medicine amazes and literally inspires.

When it comes to supporting the body and its healing powers, it fails miserably. Out of an incomprehensible twist (maybe the first pharmaceutical salesmen did such a good of a job and had such strong beliefs in the goodness of the products), western medicine almost holistically negates the way the body heals itself. Look at my case.

In order to prepare my body for the nose operation, my whole body got filled up with antibiotics directly via infusion into my blood. Then, it got sedated. All good. Additionally, I was directed to consume even more antibiotics after the surgery. The body's response: involuntary diarrhea all through the night. It was easily seen in the feces how complete intestinal flora, living on the walls of our intestines, was being ripped out. Of course, I stopped taking those antibiotics and embraced the healing wisdom of millenniums.

Interestingly, doctors know how artificial antibiotics destroy our "good", immune system supporting bacteria along with the infectious ones. It is not the presence of "the bad" ones that makes us ill. It is a jolt in balance, when "the bad" ones overpower, overtake, outnumber "the good" ones. The dis-ease comes to put us to rest, gives us a sign to heal and rebalance our life. Health lies in a balanced approach. How, then, they still prescribe what they know is not good for us?

Don't be or get fooled. After the prescribed

antibiotics do their work, your body, not only having gone through healing and disease fight, has to additionally develop a large amount of good bacteria. Otherwise, you get sick that much easier. And that's exactly what happens to people, once they start reaching for the modern pharmaceutical medicines: a down-spiralling process of having to use more, and more often, in order to function. Look around and examine for yourself. How many people over fifty do you know that do not take any Western medicine (excluding homeopathy)?

I heartily suggest (and use) raw ginger and garlic (antibiotics, antiseptics), fresh cultured yoghurts and kefirs (probiotics – "the good" bacteria source), vitamin C, oscillococinum, kambucha tea, carrots and red leafy salads. These, among many other, are my favourites. I used them to heal severe eye injury, serious sinus infection, tropical bacteria infections, virus influenza and many quick coming colds. I urge you to find and make a list of your own. This way your body will become stronger with any/every illness you may encounter. Fact.

Larry was surprised to see that no bleeding occurred when he pulled those long, fat stuffings out of my nose just three full days after the surgery. I will tell him at our last meeting that I only took two antibiotics he prescribed.

I called Don up and said I wish to invest into my time here on the north shore. That board seems to be waiting for me. He accepted $400 humbly. He shocked me again, though. With his kindness. I only met him two days ago, yet here he was telling me he'll help me out, if I need anything any time. It is rare to hear that with heartfelt words from your closest companion, let alone "a stranger". Ocean seems to know its kind.

The board needed some repairs, so I took it to the closest surf shop. There I met Matt, who later gave me his boss's phone number. Maybe I rent a room in his house for a month.

I was sitting next to the surf shop and pondered my current financial situation. Should I be a "two board warrior" or should I continue to invest into buying a couple of more boards for such different conditions here in Hawaii?

TRUTHFULNESS

As it is.

As you will be able to see the connection between lessons learnt from surfing and their use in everyday life, I remembered that in order to adjust to the situation, one needs to use the most appropriate tool at hand. Having more tools simply means having more options to use the one, which is better suited for the task at hand. Or, you could use just one for any situation. But that is mastery. We will get to it later on. What boards would be right for me?

I have been working on an equation for determining the board's dimension relative to body size and weight. It is still not quite done, but a brief calculation showed me that a shortboard for me would be a 5'8" in length, somewhere close to nineteen inches wide and I had no clue for the thickness. The board was waiting for me less then twenty yards away from my calculation place. That one and a 8'0" for bigger waves, almost a thousand dollars and I had bought the Hawaiian quiver in a couple of days.

The things we look for are already around us. Waiting for us to realize that. Relax. Open. Let it come to you. Catch it, accept it and flow with it.

Those few sentences in brief capture the essence of a surfing experience. Are you starting to feel what surfing really is? Besides a lot of fun, of course.

I read today that scientists identified an element in a human brain cell, called magnetite. It reacts to changes in Earth's energy fields.

Minutes before reading this, I had a discussion with a shaper about fixing some small dings on the biggest board I have, the ten footer. The Waimea board. He seemed pressured, as he couldn't say if the board would be ready by Friday.

"Why Friday?" I asked. I thought it was strange he would say that, since I planned to be surfing again on Friday after a week of recovery from the surgery.

"There is a big wave front coming. Twenty feet plus."

I had no intellectual information. Is this how I can feel swells? Through what they call "magnetite"? How could I use it with full awareness when surfing? How could I use it on land to flow where the expression of my being would be effortless? How could I teach others to learn this already possessed skill?

"What age are you?" she asked.

"Well, my body is made of elements constituting Earth for billions of years and were, prior to that, probably just dust in the universal wind. Now, my mind has been with me for quite some time too.

Actually, it is hard to determine my mind's age, as it seems childish in one moment, and obsessively stuck by a desire not to change, at other times."

"Who in the name are you?" she insisted on a straightforward answer. "I am most likely to be the same as you. So, no need to argue with yourself any longer. You wish to dance?" She did.

I saw Larry again today. The last before final visit. He took some stitches out from the inside of the nose and answered a couple of questions. It is nice when someone gives you a fair, straightforward answer. This way you can at least do something with the facts you get. Otherwise it is just polite "human singing".

I could go scuba diving, he said. I will not have the right nostril bigger for the rest of my life, which is a relief. I wasn't looking for a real plastic surgery, if you know what I mean. He did also tell me to allow at least ten days after surgery before going surfing. No specific reason. Maybe the chance of an infection, maybe something else. I wonder what the ocean will tell me on Friday, since the waves are already getting quite big.

It is a new life indeed. I asked Larry to tell me his personal, laid-back view of how bad my right nostril was blocked. On a scale from 1 to 10. Nine, he said.

"I can't imagine how you've breathed through only one nostril for all this time."

Well, I thought, I did practice a lot of movement, yoga and surfing in that time.

It is clear now how those areas of life where analytical, reasoning assessment should be involved, down-spiralled in my years on 'one-side nose breathing'. Money matters, a sense of identity, rational approach to projects, even respecting common sense in personal relationships. I couldn't, for example, quite figure out for the best of me why I let a woman, with whom I envisioned my whole life from the moment I saw her, simply fade out of my life. Yes, I did fall in love at first, but that grew into true love really fast. Absolutely, I supported her, and I wholeheartedly still do, in her decisions, but without rationality at all. I even supported the decisions that were obviously working against our getting close again.

Love is blind to the mind. It is not blind to the heart. A nose unblocked, the brain awaken, I see now these words are a reminder of lessons well learnt. It is now my wish to pass them on and enable those who are approaching points in their life to have the power of choice.

If you are oblivious to the problem, how will you face it and solve it if you don't even see it?

The same would go for other fields of life, where a balance between the intuitive connectedness and wisdom of logic would come in handy. Literally.

When going surfing, this is what happens first. One stands on land, where one assumes to have some degree of control over the events occurring around him. At least one believes to be in control of her or his actions and reactions. No one is super-imposing forceful surroundings. On land, one could feel that life's situations can be paused or wait for one to be ready to respond.

As soon as one leaves land and enters the ocean that changes immediately. On land, it is easy to think about the past and worry about the future. When you enter the ocean, you enter the present moment.

The ocean will not wait, respond or accustom to our needs and whims. It is there and it has its own rhythm. The ocean does not need us there. We choose to enter. As in life, we choose to enter a situation.

Our feet leave the solid ground and we swim into the ocean. With faith, we paddle into a vast, powerful space hoping to realize our desire to ride waves. Instantly, the focus shifts to the present movements of the surfboard. What is our reassurance that the ride will happen? What are we equipped with?

A small piece, infinitely small from the ocean's perspective, of a floatation device, a paddling device, which are our even smaller palms of the hands, and the will not to give up. It is astonishing how that relates to our life on land.

We have the tools we use to handle life's numerous situations. From logic to intuition to social networks and informational flows. Those are our surfboards. Then, we have our feet. And we walk. Regardless of how much you use all sorts of vehicles to get around this planet, the basic movement we use is walking. Ever such a long journey starts with the first step and continues on with one step at a time. It goes for projects, long or short in chronological time. All events humankind undertakes consist of the sequence of one step after the other. That's our paddling in this vast, powerful space of one's life journey. Lastly, and most importantly, there's our will.

I will do that. I am doing that. The will comes from a conscious or unconscious knowledge that what we pursue is there for us to realize and experience.

We see a wave breaking from the beach. Even though we are aware that we cannot ride the wave we see, we have faith in the ocean and go in hoping more waves similar to that one will come by. We get to know of things possible from the outside of us or we feel it from within in life. We somehow venture in that direction with complete trust that something will happen. This becomes our will. The biggest mistake we can do is to stop paddling, to stop observing and stop waiting. It goes the same for anything in life on land that we decided to pursue. Just keep on stepping in that general direction, keep observing, be patient and the wave will come. As a wise surfer said: "There is always a wave behind (coming)."

We draw experience into our reality and that's

why we determine with our desire and focus what types of waves are going to come our way. Yes, we don't get a second chance in the sense that every wave gone is gone. It is not coming back. They are all different from each other. But a chance for us to catch a ride, from where we are, will come again. If we learnt something from the time we had missed that first wave, that chance, and to this one, we will not only catch this chance, but we will also ride the wave even better than the missed one. That's what it means to learn from mistakes. It means to do the thing better next time around. We always get a second chance.

Why should we care about what we eat as long as we're not hungry? Because research is proving what we probably always knew anyway. You are what you eat - literally! The food choices you make, create your energy, your ability to maintain it while surfing, recover from an intense session or full day in the water so you can charge even harder the next time. The effect of food over time becomes crucial.

I wasn't happy with the new place to live that I chose. It wasn't the little Chihuahuas, since I love dogs. It wasn't the mess laying around everywhere. I rearranged my room into a creative space. It wasn't the price, which was the same as a price of a two-bedroom studio in a less "convenient" location. It was something else. It still is, and I can't put the finger on it. I will focus on finding a nicer place to stay without telling this to the landlord. He is a nice guy. A type I especially admire. Sticks to himself and speaks when necessary. Being too laid back, though, can be frustrating too.

The day, in spite of realizing how I put myself into a place where I don't feel inspired to live, has been one for which I came to Hawaii in the first place. A breakthrough in surfing.

The shaper finished in time and the big wave board got repaired. The swell came in overnight.

Leaving my bicycle at the backpackers last night, left me dependent yet again, so I enjoyed a big breakfast, knowing that Matt wouldn't be ready so early. We were supposed to go and surf the Bay together.

I meditated and waited. Nine o'clock. Ten o'clock. So many waves ridden already. But, as I said to Matt later, I knew there where waves out in the ocean that had our names written on them. It was just a matter of time.

"My back. I don't know man. The doctor said I shouldn't really put pressure on it." Matt pondered his options.

"Well, you don't have to go. Do as it feels best." the new housemate channelled.

"Ah, what the hell. Let's do it!"

And we did.

Matt got a twenty-five feet wave (8 meters). The biggest of his life so far. Me? I caught and made it to the bottom of a wave of similar, or slightly bigger (8-10m) wave, but couldn't make the bottom turn. I somehow lost control over the board, fell off and embraced an intense wipeout. The results were loose muscles and a board broken into pieces. It is a board I am the happiest to break of all broken boards. Check it out.

I told Matt we had nothing to lose and that it was, symbolically, a nice day to die. So, when I decided to paddle for my first wave, of size 8-10 meters, there was no doubt in my mind that I will successfully make that wave. Knowing that, I got faced with a predicament when attempting to make it down to the bottom of the wave, while being suspended in air and negotiating two airdrops. I succeeded. A crucial thing also happened on that take-off. The inside (right) fin got torn out of the board. I know this to be true, because the board shifted to the side when I laid on it in the lineup later on.

The second wave's scenario was the same as the third one, which eventually broke the board and ended the session. I was looking for a reason for falling off on the second wave and just could not understand why. I am glad now that I did not check the bottom of my surfboard. That's how I caught an even bigger wave, fell off at doing the turn and the rest is history.

When we stay in the moment, stay at peace with what is happening, and do our best, life will decide, when it is best for us not to know something. I believe we do not possess moral power to withhold the truth from each other, if we know and feel how related to our relationship or a certain situation it is. Not knowing should happen spontaneously and only for the reason of achieving what would with knowledge be impossible to achieve.

If I would have checked my board after the first wave, I am sure I wouldn't have gone after even bigger waves. Madness. Missing a right fin and attempting to realize a take-off and a bottom turn on a ten meter right hand wave is craziness. Yet, not knowing enabled me to be free of that problem.

After the second wave, I looked for a reason in my coordination and wave knowledge. Nothing. The problem wasn't me and I stopped worrying. Focused on the moment.

Now, the last, third wave was incredible, if you see it from a finless point of view. Yes, some boards have only one centre fin, but that design is different and the center fin is really big. I executed the take-off all the way to the lower parts of the wave. Where I started to draw an angled line, the ride ended in a memorable wipeout for the audience.

Did I make that wave? Can I say I caught a ten meter wave at Waimea?

Personally, yes. I will carry with me the feeling of a successful ten meter wave.

Publicly? What do they know, anyway? I mean, how many surfers would even make it to the lower parts of the wave without the crucial fin?

Achievements are personal. You know what you've gone through to get to where you are. No one can ever take that away from you. You don't need other people's approval of your victories. Neither do I. It is time to party. Merry Christmas!

Paul. Dave. Ariane. Nick.

Life speaks to us through the people we meet on our way. If we'd be able to hold a certain perspective, we would never need to read a book. Our circumstances are the writings on the wall. Life is already showing us how and where to go next. It is already revealing our biggest illusions, thus fear associated with those issues. It is all ready.

Raul owns a property in Ecuador and has expressed himself to the point: "Someday we can build a surf camp on that property." No. Not just a surf camp, but a camp teaching us how to live, evolved around board sports of surfing, skating and snowboarding. Food grown on the property, a skate park, workshops. That was last night. As if that's important.

Dave and I shared a ride when making my way to the airport to meet Ariane. He is starting a business on the side in Canada this year. He will take people to Vancouver Island for the weekends, teach them surfing and help them reconnect with nature. It seems he might use the method of teaching how to surf and live that I've been evolving for ten years.

Nick appeared as an angel.

Ariane had a gift for him from a friend in Brazil, so he came to the airport. He offered either a prepaid hotel room or a drive up to the north shore. It was Ariane's choice and I see now why she chose the latter.

Nick's eyes shined with youth as he enjoyed a vegan taro burger at Shark Cove's Grill. He hasn't been up here for a while. He loved the trip. He also pointed out what we all know, yet seem to forget on daily basis: "The only thing true in life is change." In Nick's words: "Life is like a book. You have the front and the back cover. Everything else in between is change."

The more we try to resist that fundamental truth, the more we suffer in one way or another. When it comes to the human experience, which allows us to experience the awareness to become aware of Oneself, another thing becomes apparent: being aware of a change creates evolution. The change for the better.

The only thing we really have in our life as possession is time. I am not speaking of chronological time, since that is an illusion. We'll get to that later.

I am referring to time as a number of possibilities to live our life. You can only do as much in one day. How many and what way we do them is determined by our vitality/energy. More creates more and less means less.

Wouldn't it be normal, logical, expected to progress in something, the more you do it? Or is it normal, logical, expected to surf for such and such period of life and stagnate?

We all know the answer and looking the other way does not solve us from being responsible. Look at the word: response – able.

Responsibility is not a moral issue. It is a skill or capacity to respond to the consequences of our actions. That's why we will always be responsible no matter what. The reflections of our actions show us if we are benefiting or obstructing. The real question is:

How fully are you able to respond?

It is logical to expect that the "older" you are, the longer you have lived, easier it would be to live. I mean, you must have learnt a lot by now.

Fact 1: depends, if really important things were studied

Fact 2: responibility determines the capacity to internalize

It is impossible to learn if you do not assume full responsibility.

Before coming to Hawaii, Ariane cleared a big confusion I had, when it came to relationships, especially with women. She put it somehow like this:

"You are not responsible for my feelings, my actions and for the lessons I need to learn. You cannot be responsible. It is impossible. So, let me do what I feel it's best for me and you do the same for yourself."

This way we can let life teach us what we need to learn in this moment. We are to each other angels only when and if we assume full responsibility for what we do/feel/say/think/are at that specific moment. This way there can never be personal conflicts or delusions. It is simply what it is.

Surfing is amazing in that aspect as well.

Entering the impersonal arena of the ocean, we are the ones who carry personal attitude. The ocean has no personal interest to do this or that to us. We choose what time, where and how we enter it.

Whatever feelings and/or thoughts are being provoked in us, are reflections of the areas of our personality that we need to address. Are being addressed.

It is not the tide, the swell, the mind, other people, the board, the, the, the, ... It is you. It is always you. Whatever you bring into the ocean, the ocean turns around and shows it to you. The sessions you will have, are going to be reflections of your awareness.

Hint: best sessions happen when we enter without any other expectation but to have fun.

Can you relate that to entering situations on land? Maybe even at the start of each new day?

The photo sequence of the last wave at Waimea Bay made it onto Surfline's feature article.

Surfline is the world's most known on-line surf hub, excelling with its forecasting models. News, techniques, competitions, lifestyle, equipment, development, surf camps and excursions, weather. It is all on Surfline.

Not a lot of surfers get into the photo articles. Well, a lot of surfers don't share the elements of my story.

I was thinking, if I should share this so-called achievement with friends and family in Slovenia. Just a few. Before clicking "send" in gmail, I asked the aloha spirit, if I am sharing this with joy in this moment. The answer was yes. Click.

The next morning I received a call from my best friend, and essentially the surf buddy from the beginning of my surf story, who lives in Fuerteventura, Canary Islands. He called to make sure I'm alright. We shared laughter over the facts of that session. We also talked about a chance of me going to Canary Islands after Hawaii.

Fortunately, he agreed to pay me for teaching at his surf house, which means I have a job starting in February. What a job! To teach wisdom of surfing to fellow Slovenians, who come to stay under the same roof for a week, ten days, two weeks, whatever they choose.

Marko asked me, if I could ask someone what Manawai means in Hawaii. That's the name of the surf house. He's explaining it as the spirit, the power of water. I met Maui the same day. This is what he had to lecture:

"The word Hawaii is comprised of three words: ha–wai–i. "Ha" can be taken as "a breath of life", although in this particular combination it means "to be created for". "Wai" means the spirit of fresh water. "I" means to go up.

Putting it all together, one could interpret that Hawaii got created for "gods" with the spirit of fresh water. This spirit, however, has a brother/sister/soulmate, whatever you wish to name the other side of polarity, which is essential for unity.

The other one is called "Kai" – the spirit of salt water, the ocean. They always work together.

Mana means more than just power or spirit. It is the essence of beings. There is a place on Oahu ("gathering place") called by the traditional, local, people Waikonu – "welcoming waters"."

Oddly, Waikonu sounds similar to welcome. Go figure.

The wave I caught at Waimea Bay on Christmas 2009 changed my life. Period.

The first thing it created was a reality for me to become a witness in my own story. I feels humbled by the reality that Jernej manifested. It proved to me that everything Jernej followed and believed in to be true. The way he nurtured his body with food, water, salt and thoughts. The way he trained his body by breath, internal vitality and focus. The way he meditated the enlightened spirit. The way he mediated peace and joy to others. The way he studied energy, water and the interaction of both in surfing. It all proved to be creative.

Five years of surfing experience. A week after the nose surgery, when he healed the body with meditation and using only natural medicine. The biggest wave of the day without a fin.

Put your life in perspective. Step outside of your mind and who you think you are. Simply observe what your life is like. Admire. Be grateful.

The second thing that happened on that wave was the photographer's success in capturing it. This enables some positive catalytic changes in people of utmost importance for the future. Publishing the photo on Surfline is just a part of the puzzle. Time will tell.

The third thing that happened became clear tonight. Simon, the landlord of the house I am staying at, asked me, if I feel comfortable and if everything is alright with my stay. I said, everything is not as I though it would be. We went on to show the world, how a conflict is a constructive venture and how things can be discussed by being open and sharing. We not only resolved the issues of laundry and internet connectivity, but also gave each other the chance to grasp the view of why we met.

Amongst many things, irrelevant for these pages, he told me that the surfer with whom I shared that wave at Waimea is his protégé. He taught him almost everything he knows about surfing the north shore.

I haven't showed him my tattoo writen with Japanese characters yet, although I am sure he is able to read it.

His son is toying with an idea to focus on being a professional athlete, a surfer in this case. I offered to share the wisdom of training the body with the mind through the spirit. You know, even you probably perceive professional athletes to be in perfect health. That, in my own experience and research, is far from reality.

Their bodies are usually fed with "unhealthy" food, primarily being focused on the quantity of the energy output, rather than the quality of inner vitality and ways to generate and manage internal energy flow. Their minds might be, or not, calmer as a result of years of intense mental practice. It might, which is often the case, make them emotionally fragile. Feeling empty, when losing and full, when winning.

Competition is about overcoming your limits and excelling, not about comparing yourself with others. That's for the audience.

Somehow. Someone. The information about surfing has found me. I saw it on the internet. Someone was flipping a magazine on a bus. There was a poster I noticed. I heard two people talk and she said: "No, no, no, that's windsurfing. This is surfing. No sails, just the wave and energy of the ocean." It got me curious. An activity using only your body and a simple board. Seems like you have to be well connected to use waves in the ocean to have so much fun. One day I am doingthat. Learning how to stay connected and have fun at the same time.

The more you educate yourself in as many fields of the human experience, the more you open the span of possibilities that you can realize.

A professional athlete would have to know every little detail about how the body works, its interaction and influential relationship with the mind, how to use the spirit to enhance body/mind relation, besides knowing "the rules of play" of the chosen sport. After all, the body is the tool in the game of sports.

I went for a sunset session at Sunset. It clearly showed me what I was to experience later that evening while talking to Simon. The problem always lies inside us. Never outside. Read on.

As I surfed the famous, powerful spot of Sunset for the first time, I approached it with a student's attitude. Let me see where the waves break, how the lines on the horizon travel, where people wait, how the energy from the neighbouring breaks affects it.

I observed a lot of things. Actually, so many that I forgot to watch for a way in which I could catch one of those waves. This oblivion to the task I initially went in to do, lead simply to the fact of being caught on the inside three times in thirty minutes. In surfing we say one gets caught inside when the waves break onto/in front of the surfer and push her/him towards the shore, so that they have to paddle a long way to get back to where they were. Sometimes, as in the case of Sunset, this can mean five minutes of intense, strenuous paddling. Just because you didn't observe well.

I almost got frustrated, but quickly realized that there wasn't any problems outside of me. I was simply in the wrong spot at the right time. The worst outcome was a little bit more paddling exercise. Training is good.

It seems as Simon somehow sensed I might have a problem with my stay here. There were trains of thoughts going through my mind in the last few days. It all seemed to revolve about money, price of rent and the value I saw appropriate for the money asked. How foolish, yet we learn every day.

COURAGE

To be who I am.

When money gets stuck onto an experience, service, object or anything, the thing apparently gets value. Apparently, because it is subjectively stupid.

Everyone values a rock according to their needs and disposable money. Thus, outside of all those people the rock stays a rock.

The first thing that money does is devalues gratitude towards what we have, instead of what we should be having. But I paid honest money for it! Craziness. Example.

If I go and buy a thousand dollars worth big wave board, then go out, catch a fifteen meter wave, ride it, go for another one, fall, break the board, would that mean the wave was worth a thousand dollars?

It is impossible to put value onto experience. No matter what or who enables it. That's why gratitude is invaluable, since it brings infinite joy into one's life. Was the wave worth nine hundred dollars? Get out of here.

As in surfing, so in life.

To put it into a statement that is what I am saying.

Whatever creates a joyful session in the ocean has got the power to create a fulfilling life when practiced on land.

Keep this in mind or perspective, as I'll draw lessons learnt from playing in the ocean and implement them in life's situations, so you could see this clearly. Truth seems to resonate in us, regardless of the symbolic language we perceive it in.

Let us take the principle act of surfing – a wave ride.

In order for me to catch a wave, I need to be in a certain place at a certain time. I need to be where the wave will come and start breaking. So in life.

If you wish to realize something, you need to put yourself in a situation where it would be possible to realize it. You need to be in a certain place at a certain time. How do I get there?

I get there by waiting for the swell to come and by going to a place where waves will break, where they have broken in the past or where it is extremely likely for them to break in the future. You don't go to a CD shop to buy a hemp bag. Observe where chances are for you to realize what you have set out to.

Next, it is not enough for me to simply be where the wave will come. When it does, I still need to catch it. I need to paddle for it and find an entry point. Nothing is given without will. Possibilities appear around you and if you go after them, they turn into chances.

Then I get to my feet and the ride begins. You get your chance and realize your dream the best way you can at that moment. If I fall, or wipeout as surfers say, I just have to go back, wait, observe better, learn and do it again. On account of a lesson learnt from a mis-take, I get another take with a better chance to make it. You always get another chance. If you have learnt something, it will be easier the next time around.

Waves come and go. That is the nature of life.

There is no logical or emotional reason for me to wish for that wave to come back. I can, on the other hand, rejoice in the wisdom that the wave I will ride is already travelling towards me through the ocean of space and time.

What you have wished to do is already being created. Give it time, let it come, observe, paddle for it and take the leap of faith. There is no trying. You do it or you don't.

Learning and growth are consequences of courage. Courage is the absence of wisdom. Wisdom comes from experience. Experience gives you the freedom to recognize, realize. This is the way to spiral connectivity.

Sun will keep on shining. Swells will keep on happening. Waves will keep on breaking. You will keep on having chances to realize your potential.

Nothing is wasted, as long as it is tasted.

It is 31st of December 2009. It is 1st of January.

As our civilization revolves around the sun, the way we organized our culture essentially resembles Earth's rotation. Day and night dictate what we have called time. There is a view of a wave in this that I wish to share here with you. Aloha.

Imagine Earth as it spins around. From the perspective of one day, the sun seems to be in one place of the universe. It is the earth's rotation that makes us believe and see as if the sun travels the sky. Still, there are places on land that are still in the dark. Places onto which the sun shines and places slowly disappearing into the night. Imagine a wave of light that travels around the globe. In front of the wave, animals and people mostly rest. When the wave comes, people get up from a laying position, as flowers they reach towards the sun, and go running around, living the day, until they lay down to rest after the sun sets behind the horizon.

What is special about the transition in a calendar year are all those wishes, projections, desires, needs that people fill their heart's and mind's vibration with for the following 360 and some days. A chance for a bigger change.

So it travels. As the time difference affects when people celebrate the transition, it is a twenty-four hour wave of wishing to change for the better. That's why, I take deep consideration on what I wish for the future to bring into my present on 31st of December. My personal new year is my birthday, while a calendar year holds globally transforming potential.

May we all be like water babies in the new year.
May we flow back to and recognize the universal
source.
May we treat water as this planet's most valuable
re-source.
May we adapt instantly, as water does.
May we flow smoothly around any obstacle that comes
on our path,
Yet keep our goal clear and eventually dissolve the rock.
Water is the universal solvent. The solution lies in
water's wisdom.
May we reflect naturally, as water does.
May we flow effortlessly, as water does.
May we enjoy this magnificent planet and
May we realize that it is blue, without having to be sad.
May we be like water.

Ariane and I took a trip to Napali Coast today. We didn't get to it, but that's OK. Different than most of the people, we tend to pay attention to the journey, rather than just focusing on the end goal. Being somewhere else on the way.

Which lead me to think about surfing again.

As the wave's dance is so captivating. As the ride is so enjoyable. As everything flows in motion without interference or pause, the wave ride puts you immediately in the present moment.

One learns that the mere act of thinking, that is connecting thoughts in a logical sequence, results in the end of the ride or a mistake. Interruption in fluidity. The connection gets lost with the wave and the surfer finds herself/himself outside of the present moment. The focus is on the very ride at that time and place.

How the ride will end or what will happen at the end of the ride or what the reward is or what will I do after the end? All of that does not exist when you actually ride the wave. All of that comes of itself when it needs to. There is no luxury of worrying about it. It is just the ride.

Step by step we go through life. Do you notice magic on the way or do you stare at the goal while life passes you by?

There's no real pressure. No real need to do, be, say or act. It comes with such ease. You develop and grow simply because you are curious. You want to know more. You want to taste the earth. You want to crawl better, sit longer and be awake more. It is an essential part of your being - evolution. The body is growing fast and you need to keep pace with all this fresh information that is allowing you to experience. No trying. Only doing. No pressure. Situations present themselves so vividly. All you need to do is continue playing.

We stood on the edge of the path. Ariane said she wanted to give me something. I knew it was a game. We played. She bent over and started picking up something. The inquisitive mind went "Is it a flower I don't know?", "Is it a special thing?", "Is it...?", "What if..." I smilingly observed the child at play. She lifted a rock and said:

"Here. This is for you. I give this to you."

I accepted the rock. "Thank you." I played along, curious what could happen next.

"Do you like it?" Ariane asked.

"Well, it's a rock."

"But, do you like it?"

"I don't take things from nature that I don't need."

"What will you do with it?"

It seemed natural to leave it in nature, where it belongs.

The whole interaction inspired me to see how we gravitate to either being a giving or a receiving person. Which makes no sense. They are both a part of one process.

When you give, you have to be willing to receive. When you receive, you agree to give. It was something else that made me realize how foolish we are when not understanding the practical side of receiving and giving.

When the play of energy gives me a wave, it is simply not like that at all. It does not give it, it just is. The fact that I am there creates the situation of giving and receiving. As I do something, which is valuable to you, it has nothing to do with you, but everything to do with me, the ocean.

You can be grateful, feel lucky or whatever you call it, that you were there. Both of us do not know why. The ride, or time on land, will show us both how my giving and your receiving benefited us both.

Now. Back to catching a wave. Think of it as a gift. You receive an energy wave that travelled x thousand miles, interacted with the ocean floor just right, so you can ride it. You receive. Yet, you have no idea, what you are receiving. It is impossible for you to foresee how the wave will break and the ride it will manifest. You trust. Why don't you do it on land as well?

When you have a feeling to give or help someone, why not simply ask if you can help in any way or do something? Even if you don't foresee how.

Why not receive with gratitude, even if you don't have an idea, how the help/ride/act may turn out in the end? You would be surprised by the outcomes of such interactions.

Max is the landlord of the hostel in Kaapa, where we rented a room for the time of our stay in Kauai. He told Ariane that they call tonight's full moon a Blue moon. It is supposed to happen every twenty years. I am curious to find out more, because it happens to be a new year's eve. 2009 to 2010. When was the last time two numbers created a year date, one being half the value of the other, and both sharing a similar form (2-0, 1-0)?

Max also explained, what aloha means to him.

"It's how I feel." Well said.

We went again. Into the rainforest of the wettest part of the island. The familiar trail to Kalalau. Barefoot, like yesterday.

People walk all day long along the lush hills and

through pristine rivers. Never really getting in touch. Protected from the sun. Shielded from air with clothes. Most ironically, separated from the earth by layers of footwear. Water. Stones. Mud. Aqua detox. Foot massage. Skin peeling. For free. Walking slowly like this, wishing not to fall or hurt our feet, forced us to enjoy every step. We didn't make it as far in body as the rest. We came far in spirit and what we'll take with us from the two trips to H'aena State park.

We met quite a few people on the trail. Some got enchanted by Ariane, some fell into the ocean in Jernej's eyes. We got touched by everyone.

His name was Daniel. He seemed to have come to walk this trail in order to experience the old traveller's saying: "Pack only what you can carry." Daniel packed way too much. Still, he was determined to make it back to the parking lot without help. We could only offer our company.

In return, he offered me an inspiration for today's writing. It is on social interaction.

How we approach people that we randomly meet. Not having a predetermined fixation on how long our interaction lasts, people seem to open without fear when on a journey. Since there is no obligation, there is no tension. There are no pre-tensions.

Funny, isn't it? If you consider that our life is a journey, every moment of it. What obligations do you feel you have towards me?

That's right. The same ones as I have towards you.

Honesty. Fairness. Respect.

Honest to be who I am.

Fair to do what I feel/think is right.

Respect you for who you are and what you do.

Amazingly enough, in an ambience of these virtues, people do not tend to harm or take advantage.

The internet account balance showed three transactions, which I was sure I did not make. They summed up to one thousand Australian dollars. Upon doing some currency conversion, it became obvious how at least one transaction matched the rental car expense. Could it be that the other big one paid the mechanical repair of the car?

One the first day of the rental period, the car started making noises in the gearbox area. Better to change it. It later turned out to be a fatal decision for my camera, as it got left behind. They still hadn't called me.

People just take what isn't theirs and then wonder how come they never get enough. You take, it is taken. You give, you receive.

I studied the contract. Should have read the small print.

Over dinner, Ariane offered a great conversational playground and we explored my financial background. Whenever I had a surplus of money, I would spend it as fast as possible. Sure, my expenses were not some ridiculous "out-of-my-lifestyle" pleasures. They all have made sense. The real question is: "Where is the key to enable this experience, but in a more affordable way?"

The question was answered the next day as we rode the bus from Waikiki to the north shore of Oahu.

I found it funny. Almost "high-schooly". She was posing next to the statue. As did many other tourists on the Waikiki walking strip. Then it hit me. I had tremendous respect for Duke Kahanamoku out of the history research I did. He is one of the priests of Hawaiian spirits. An embodied ambassador of Aloha.

On a physical level, he is still the only surfer in the world honoured with a statue, where people from all walks of life, from all around the world, take pictures with him. And they feel honoured.

Think about that. As far as I know, the only surfer in the world with a statue.

Money almost stole my creativity. Almost, because I see now how having more than I needed stopped me from searching a non-financial or simply cheaper way to realize something. Interestingly, when being broke, I would somehow always find a solution to get back on track. I was broke many times. It is something I don't fear. It puts you in a very survival-like state and defines your advantages while painfully challenges your limitations.

Being creative does not only mean you do something you like or you find it easy to do. Being creative essentially means to know how to turn a useless situation into a purposeful one. It is challenging to be creative, yet it is based on the principle of fun. Even those who claim to be creative under extreme pressure/stress can honestly realize that the idea comes when they give up and relax the mind.

How can you be creative under fear?

Another big swell is on the way. As I've stated, it might be one of the biggest in the modern recorded history. I am here to ride big waves. That is one of my goals for Hawaii. I need a proper board. Again.

There is a month and a week left of my stay here. Having to pay the remaining $600 to Liam for my rent until 25th of January leaves me with $800. Big wave boards cost anywhere from $400 to $700. I do have money in my European account, but I decided not to spend from it anymore for the living expenses. It is there for a reason. A reason which is in the future and I cannot yet see.

Time to get creative. This is what Ariane and I talked about when riding the bus.

One idea was to post a donation on FB saying: "If you believe in what I inspire you, would you then be willing to share some of your energy with me? I am collecting money to buy a big wave board for the next big swell." Etc ... Something in that line.

Another idea was to find someone who would fix my old board for $160. We were on a roll.

I realized how having the power to buy whatever I needed without effort disabled me to be creative. Don't get me wrong. I am by no means a billionaire. Yet, I am lucky to have simple needs, such as surfboards and tickets being the most expensive ones. Lucky to be without any debt and with a couple of thousand Euros in the account.

What's relevant now is how fast life tells us if we are on the path of continuos growth or if we are in our own, so believed, comfort zone.

When on the first one, "good" things happen. Synchronicity. Connection. I guess you know well enough about the comfort zone. Problems never end.

We got back to the north shore in the late afternoon. Simon and the boys just came back from a session. The wind turned and it got messy. Should have been here an hour ago. Classic.

They were all happy with the waves they got. Without any hint whatsoever about what I had planned to do for the big wave board project, Simon said I could use his brother's 10'6". He showed me the board. Shaped by Stretch. Quad fin setup. Classic.

All I needed was to buy four fins. Sixty to seventy bucks. If I break it, I pay five hundred. No risk, no fun.

I asked Simon what he thinks about repairing

my other gun, classic 80's board.

"That board needs to go in the bin out in front of the house." Respects were paid to it. I put it there today.

Search yourself before deciding on what you wish to materialize. It could be anything. Then, hold your vision. Don't ever give up. Believe. Trust. Let it happen. It always does. It always will.

A month or so ago. Maui. Val and I woke up in the dark. We left the house at first light. She had a feeling that a spot thirty-minute ride away might be working really well. A session with a friend and good waves. Ah, that's what it is all about.

People do have similar ideas. We were by no means the first ones there. Actually, quite a few people were already surfing. We decided to check some other spots. Only to fulfill one of unwritten surf trip rules: "If you check a spot and it's good, you will always end up at the same spot, regardless of how many others you go to see."

In between, we caught the morning traffic. Or it caught us. Val had surf lessons to do, which gave us an hour to surf. No problemos! There's plenty of time to get waves in an hour. Yeah, if there are any waves!

It had to be the longest lull, a period without incoming waves when surfers wait, in Maui. The whole hour. It was time to go in and go to work. I gave in. Murphically, the set came when I was close to the beach. That means, the whitewater of the broken wave tumbled me about for a while and eventually washed me onto the rocky beach.

Val did get one wave. Of course she did, since her real name in English literally translates into a wave in the Slovenian language.

Sometimes we enter a situation without expectations. We still get shocked by what happens. No waves for an hour! However, we laugh hysterically every time we remind ourselves of that bizarre morning. Waking up early, checking spots, caught in traffic, an hour lull.

We did not lose, but gained. It is like this most of the time. Even when our mind tells us how insane it is. Embracing the unknown.

Watched Pipeline for two hours, while recording the essence of the wavergy method for surfing. I had a meeting with Dave at ten o'clock, where I explained what he could expect to listen in the two hour recording. Dave is planning to have a surf school in Canada and he wishes to use this method.

Gone looking for fins to put on the 10'6" Simon offered for me to borrow. Waimea will break tomorrow. Wind stays a mystery. There are three more swells on the way. It is turning to be the best season for big waves in twenty years. Eddie is here.

Here's an example by Jernej to demonstrate how assumption is the cause of all misunderstandings. When Simon offered the board, he simply said: "You'll have to get some fins for it." He meant exactly what he said and Jernej "the wise" assumed he meant he did not have any at the shop for, oh Jernej, to buy. So, the "Journey" went on the search for an entire day, looking for the right type of fins for the board. He came back with two sets of plastic fins, which he doubted were any good for the occasion.

He felt the urge to ask Simon for advice if he got the right fins for that board. Well, the right ones were waiting at Simon's shop for $85. Great assuming, Jernej!

Here's the catch, though: had Jernej bought those fins, they wouldn't searched through the fins in the house and they wouldn't have talked about Jernej's approach to body/mind training and nutrition. On the other hand, if Jernej would buy the fins from Simon's shop, he would have the right ones and they would simply find another situation for the talk. Who knows?

One thing is for certain. I need to drink that noni juice based medicine Simon told me about. I need to cure this nose. What happened?

I got hit in the nose with a surfboard ten days after the surgery and the body created a swelling inside to protect the injury. There is a chance for the swelling to calcificate and turn into a bone. That would mean, I'd be back with breathing through one nostril. No way Jose, whoever you are!

COMPASSION

Whatever I do to you, I do to myself.

Ariane was right: "You can have whatever whenever."

Don gave me some clothes he got for free. I just got sponsored by aloha spirit. Waimea Bay was fun, relaxing and small today. Only four meters. How a view changes through personal experience. Per-spective. A point of view.

When a day like today happens, a mind trick is necessary, if I wish to capture its essence and express it through words to you.

If it is just you, it is you anyway.
We are so soul-made.

These sayings were going through Ariane's and Jernej's heads. They were walking home to Rocky Point on the night bike path, smiling in their hearts under the star-filled sky. They are there all the time. Stars. People to give us a hand when we give one.

The first car, on an otherwise empty road in Haleiwa at ten past ten, stopped. We had been hitch-hiking all day. That was our transport of choice for the whole day. This one took us right to home.

We came from Mike's place. Ariane has a new tattoo. She actually said, riding in the back of a pick-up truck after tattooing that she feels it has always been a part of her. As if it was meant to be there. Now, it certainly is. Once things happen, they happen. Point of no return. That's why it is said it is wise to think twice.

Not that thinking in itself would be wise. A lot of people do that. It is acting upon wisdom. That's why it is good to "think twice". So we get a chance to see correctly, both sides, intuitive and rational.

I honour and respect Mike's approach to doing tattoos. He is one of few people around the world I met and recommend their service. He not only works with his heart, but with a very sound based rational approach. Based on truth. Love and truth.

When things change, they change. When you get a tattoo done, it is there to stay. As Mike said: " You can get a laser treatment done, but the scar of the tattoo we do will stay."

Mike engraves your skin to be ornamented until you meet your grave. He understands that completely. Offering a very personal experience is what he offers. Explores the real intentions behind your desire, design, idea. What is it you are wishing to express through a tattoo? "Happiness is a big part of it," he said. "Communication and direction," he summed up what enabled Ariane to get a tattoo.

When we got to Mike's place something didn't look good from the moment I saw him. A few minutes later, I was observing attentively to find the problem.

He was explaining to Ariane, how he wasn't one hundred percent satisfied with his sketches and the research on the image of the flower. He did look and examine the images we gave him, but they didn't prove informative enough.

"If I had a name or we knew more about this flower/plant ... Or we had more time ... Or ... Or ..." I decided to do as I do in the surf.

There I was listening to him about what he felt and thought. It didn't look and sound good. I was sitting in the line-up and observing the ocean. Where's the wave?

I saw an opportunity coming. Mike was finishing his speech. Ariane was neutral; not wishing to give up, not wishing to force.

I said: "Would you be willing to give me fifteen minutes and I'll search for the name, and we'll take it from there."

Mike answered: "Sure. Go for it."

To which I replied: "You know, I don't wish to create any kind of pressure. If I find some images and a name, that's cool. If I don't, fine. There is no need for you to do anything you don't like. I'm just paddling for a wave. I might catch it and get a ride or I might wipeout." The name. The photo. Cleared misunderstanding. Symmetry. Simplicity. Mandala.

Ariane's explanation of the insight for it.

The central point of the mandala represents a "space" where everything that exists comes from and where everything is bound to return to. This space is, at the same time, the beginning, the end and the way. It is the common "place" that connects everything to every little thing in the Universe.

We all - humans, rocks, plants, water, mosquitoes, visible or invisible beings etc. – we all rose from there and we will all go back to that place of complete harmony again when the material journey transmutes. While incarnated, we can reach this holy and cosmic place through spiritual practices or any activity that really has the power to align you to who you really are, in purity.

In the mandala, this mystical place is graphically represented by the central point. We can call it God, we can call it Love, we can call it Source. We can name it however it seems more suitable to level of acceptance for each one of us.

And then, if you visualize the mandala, you will see that, as an energetic chain, all that is connected to that universal central point starts expanding on and on. Endlessly. The first movement affects the following one that affects the following ones, and it goes on like this forever. Butterfly effect. Like the meetings and encounters that we live in life. Any influence your presence causes in someone is an opportunity to expand a little bit more and pass it on to whoever that comes across your path. In Nature, this movement creates just the most perfect interaction and most rhythmical dance.

In spite of the huge and eternal expansion, it never gets lost, since there is a center, a stem, which is always a safe reference to learn. Like in meditation, you expand your level of consciousness, but you never get lost, because you are connected to the most reliable divine energy, you are connected to the principle of everything.

This movement is a contradiction that makes the biggest sense ever, because while you are expanding, you are actually returning to the origin. By doing that, you are connecting yourself to your higher self and to the higher source, in order to reach Unity. Expanding, returning, expanding, returning. Like a heart's beat. The movement that keeps everything working. Alive.

So, the mandala shows this opposite, simultaneous and constant movement of expanding and returning to the source: the point that links you to the whole cosmic existence.

And it can be expanded all life long. All existence long. That is why the Universe is infinite: because it never stops expanding. As we are made by the universal substance, so we are also part of this eternal expansion.

The mandala is also circular, since the things in the Universe work in cycles. When/where one cycle finishes, another one starts from that. The end is the beginning, the beginning is the end. Like death and life. Positive and negative. Silence and sound. They travel together. One enables the existence of the other.

Life is an amazing and sacred journey towards the evolution. And the more we are connected to the center, the more we are able to expand. The more we expand, the more we connect to the center. Each one of us holds a particular inner infinite. We are all gods, love, cause and effect, masters and creators.

We are all divine beings who receive a sacred gift called Life.

We went to Paradise Found café for lunch again. Inside Celestial Foods shop. In a similar fashion as we met Mike two days ago, we met Ana in the café. She told me that I got a short clip in one of the most famous Brazilian on-line surf articles, within a movie made about Christmas day at Waimea Bay. I decided to call her husband Roberto. It was time to tell why we didn't go on a scuba-diving trip with Ariane. Reason? Simple. I got hit in my nose by a surfboard ten days after the surgery. Three days after Waimea session, and the nose is very sensitive now. And she decided to get a tattoo in her last days. It might also be an opportune time to see what was happening with our movie project.

I came to Hawaii to realize three things: make a breakthrough in my surfing; get the final insights for this book and get sponsored on account of surfing done here. For the latter, Roberto and I agreed on a personal movie project. But, it wasn't going anywhere. Until today.

He answered my phone call. I remembered it said Deep Ecology on his business card. Standing on the other side of the road, just in front of Celestial Foods, it made sense to ask: "Where are you?"

"I'm at the shop." I played a little bit.

"Is that the shop in Haleiwa?"

"Yes."

I walked across the street into the shop, came up

to the counter, looked at him and said something like: "Well, we can hang up our phones then."

He said he had a video on a Brazilian on-line site to show me. Of course. We went back to the café to eat. He looked to be in a lot of pain. What else then to admit that I can do shiatsu?

We finished our food, Ariane and I, and walked across the road to Deep Ecology's shop. Jernej became "The Healer". Meanwhile, Roberto browsed the internet and found some new photos of that big wipeout I experienced.

In the evening, I found a sequence of the first wave. The wave that took out the fin on the board. Thank you Roberto for the website address and thank you, Doug Palama, for taking those photos.

"I need to get my beard shaved first." I insisted. "We'll be on Jernej's time for the beginning."

Ariane did not oppose. We got dropped off next to McDonald's. Supposedly, there was a hairdresser close by. He had a 'barber shop' sign on display. "Sweet." I thought. Yet, he hadn't used a blade since it got prohibited because of HIV. Nevertheless, the machine did its thing and I was ready to start embracing a new beginning later on. What a day!

Pachi asked me: "Already been out?" He seemed eager to get some waves at the bay.

"Well, it's not big. And I decided to do a yoga session on the beach. At the same time, I've been given to ride this board for the swell and I noticed a ding after yesterday's session. I tested the board and since conditions are not that great..."

Pachi was already gone. A guy came by. Our eyes connected as I finished the sentence: "... and I wish to respect the board, so I didn't feel like taking it out with an open ding." The guy didn't look away. I didn't as well. Ok. I'll just explain it to you.

It was obvious to me that he believed I was making excuses not to go out for four to five meter waves.

We choose what we believe in. There's no point in arguing what someone chose. It is a choice. I just said: "Whatever."

I turned around and said to Ariane: "It's small. I get scared, when it's small."

Direction. A crucial part of development.

A plant grows upwards. Growing sideways enough to ensure its place under the sun. The river bends in the valley. It always flows downwards. Water searches for the way down. Upon reaching its destination, it starts the journey into the sky.

Direction is a big part of a human life.

One can have tremendous will and vitality. All of those might bring nothing but confusion, if direction is not applied. Direction births directive, which brings already started projects to an end. That end gives inspiration to a new start.

Think about what you could have achieved to this moment in your life if you would only finish every little or big project that you started.

One could have a steady direction to live a fuller and happier life with every passing day. Now, that is the directive I chose. It is out of this understanding that I say to people: "My life is a working holiday."

I came to enjoy, yet I also came to learn. By learning I transform what I know into what I do. Knowledge becomes wisdom. No need for beliefs and assumptions. Assumptions, especially, cause conflicts.

"Where are you from?"

"Slovenia. A small country in Europe."

"Oh, do you have waves there?"

" There are no waves you could really surf."

" So, you probably surf, when it's small here."

I did answer: "I'm from my mother" but people seem to get offended, because they don't understand. Something like, I asked you a simple question and you answered what I don't understand. There are no simple answers, only questions.

Watching Pipeline on the last day of Ariane's visit, I left the random surfer believe what he chose to believe.

What good would it do if I tried to convince him that I surfed 20-25 feet Waimea, 15 feet Puerto Escondido, 12-15 feet Sunset and 4 feet Pipeline on a 5'8"? I am thankful to him, since he inspired this part of the book.

People either possess wisdom or beliefs. They exclude each other.

If I know, not mentally, but also experientially, I don't need to believe. If I don't know, I can either choose to admit ignorance and stay open to experience or I can choose to believe whatever I find acceptable.

When someone assumes, takes for granted a fact based on personally drawn subjective conclusions, something about me, I know they choose to believe. I have no time or will or intention to argue what someone chose to believe. What sense it is to argue a choice?

The biggest swell in the world would not change a thing in surfing if it hit a coast unsuitable for surfing.

The best advice goes unnoticed when a person has no direction. The best proof does not convince someone who chooses to believe otherwise.

Experience is the best teacher.

Standing on the beach at Sunset beach today, I decided to consciously start creating my wave sessions. I was looking at a dynamic ocean and quite big waves. My wish: "I wish to exercise, train paddling technique, catch at least one big wave, get to know the spot and the board better."

Reflecting now that's what happened.

The current was strong. It almost pulled me away from where the waves were breaking. Don was already out there. An embodied spirit. A lucky charm.

He saw me drop into 12-15 footer really late. I made it. Then, the current almost took us out to sea.

Being on a 8'0" and paddling with eighty percent paddling power, my choice to end the session proved right. I was not moving at all!

I intentionally paddled away from the current towards the shore, which meant I got inside the breaking waves by doing so. Next big set gave me a thorough water massage. I finally got washed to shore.

Don came out much later. We laughed.

I told him: "None of the clothes you gave me fitted. I'll sell them to friends in Europe, where they are much more expensive."

Is that fair? To sell what you've been given? Is it fair to sell what belongs to all of us to use?

Big swells seize to finish. A 20-25 feet swell is due on Sunday/Monday. Late in the next week, an 18 feet swell is scheduled to come. Eddie is here.

I woke up quite early and checked Rocky Point. The left looked inviting. I was supposed to go surf with Matt, but he kind of liked to sleep in. It was a great chance to extend my relationship with the magical 6'8" that Don sold me.

Even though the sets were quite big and powerful, I got out with ease. The current did me a favour. Only a few moments later did I see it as an enemy. Why?

Simply because the almighty Jernej decided to stay in one spot, so he could surf the left he saw from the land.

Everything changes when you enter a situation.

The ocean in this case. The almighty Jernej did fight the ocean. But, he lost he battle.

I caught one closeout left and went in for breakfast. What did I learn?

If the current/flow is taking you somewhere you wish to go, freakin' let it take you!

You see, as I was paddling against it, I examined the breaks further down towards Pipeline, in the direction of the current. They seemed to be working good and with few people out.

Amazingly enough, I found myself surfing really crowded Pipeline two hours later. Amazingly enough, I kept watching those other good spots up towards Rockies. Amazingly enough, the current at Pipeline went the other way. Where did they meet? Amazingly enough, I overheard two local surfers talk how they'll surf wherever the current takes them. Like a ferry ride. Amazingly enough, I've learnt yet another lesson from the ocean through surfing. Amazingly enough, I've let myself go with the flow of the same day.

I saw Roberto in the evening at his home. He needs my help and I need his. I am guiding him in creating a change for the better. I am also healing him for a limited time while here. He is offering to do the movie project. He is basically supporting me to get sponsored. And, thank you for those kiwis and, especially, the two pieces of that delicious bread with butter.

Finding infinite pleasure in everyday situations keeps the spirit youthful.

All forecasts predict this next swell to hit tomorrow and stay big on Monday and get even bigger than the one for the Eddie. Ten to fifteen meter wave faces. Wind will make it impossible to surf on Sunday. Monday is staying an option. Well, might as well spend the Sunday for a day's long meditative preparation. Oh, yes, and buy fins and a leash for the board. Goes without saying.

If it's just you, it's you anyway. We are so soul-made.
Think/contemplate/reflect/observe.

"This is the most beautiful sport I've ever watched. I've been here for hours. I'm not tired or bored. It's just so amazing to watch surfers work against and with nature." The lady was telling me, as I changed my clothes.

You do wish to see people surf Pipeline one day if you go to Hawaii. You'll see why. I'll tell you why. It is the most beautiful sport to watch.

Learning how to surf involves taking off on waves. The act of catching a wave is an integral part of having the chance to ride it. Otherwise, the possibility does not exist. What happens with the ride? At the time of getting to our feet, we yet do not know. The only way to learn, though, is to do it.

Learning how to live involves accepting situations. The act of experiencing something new is integral part of having the chance to live.

Otherwise, the possibility does not appear. What happens with life? At the time of embracing a new situation, we yet do not know. The only way to learn, though, is to do it.

Think/contemplate/reflect/observe.

Waimea Bay broke in eight to ten meter range on bigger sets. It was magical. Eventful. Personally, the wave I caught cost me $500, the session offered some great lessons and again I've seen the changing power of a surfing experience.

I caught and rode one wave. My friend's board, which he let me ride saying: "If you break it, you pay $500," got broken by at least a ten meter wave. It took ten surfers out of the lineup and broke five boards. It also scared some egos out of the water.

The Hawaiian Water Patrol is worthy of my limitless respect and honour. They are true amateur professionals in the sense that they do what they do out of love for what they do. The lessons?

If you focus on what other people do or say, you will deal with the people. If you focus on the ocean/life, you will deal with that.

Whatever You focus on, defines your reality.

The turtle came three times. It showed me where to sit and wait for the next big set. But, I looked at the people to see where I would have a clean line to go without them paddling towards me or trying to go for a wave. Trying, not going. I ignored the turtle. That way I watched three empty 8 meter plus waves go through unridden or people falling, because they were too late.

I paddled into four bigger waves, but needed to pull away to avoid possible collision with fellow surfers. Waves come and go. Injuries and scars stay for some time.

Matt was maybe right. Maybe I looked to calm and it didn't seem real to people, as they were not that comfortable. I wasn't courageous. I wasn't scared. It was just me playing in the ocean. Big wave surfing maybe is something else for other people. It is just surfing for me.

As we discovered with Matt in the evening revision of the day, we go and surf Waimea, because no other spots in our neighborhood work. We don't wish to drive far. Why would we? We don't own a jet-ski. Why would we bother, when we love paddle surfing? Surfing a paddle.

I dealt with people. I somehow managed to get a wave with two other guys. Very uncharacteristic. I was also dropping in on someone. It somehow seems acceptable to people here. Unless you were having high expectations on media coverage on the beach. Then, you "had" to put on an angry-like expression and charge. Charge what? Or better, charge whom?

The wave I caught was fun. Not huge. Just fun. I thanked the lifeguard for being there on the jet-ski that day. He would take me to the beach later on.

Eventually, since what I focused on brought me more stress than fun, I went to sit among the pack, with a decision to pick a "smaller" one and finish for the day. The swell was peaking. I didn't have fun on the account of dealing with the crowd, part of which had questionable intentions to be out there and were at moments scared. I became blind together with them and did not react to the on-coming wave soon enough. Ten people and their boards got taken with a ten meter plus wave. Five boards got broken. Including mine.

It was for a reason. Thank you Waimea Bay for being a sacred place of selfish giving. May your valley be long safe from people's impact and may you show them the way. Mahalo. Wordless thank you.

Time to move into the study of the universal pattern of a spiralling motion.

Did you know that the water entering a human cell with its molecules spins the same direction as the universe does? Did you know that some say both, light and sound, spread in space in a spiralling form? Did you know that the swells we surf get created by the upward spiralling effect of the wind?

I mentioned to Matt how I'd like to focus on tube rides and turns for the rest of my stay here. I also said I would love to surf some smaller waves and not have to worry about big wave sets behind. We should simply find two to three foot waves today, where we could be alone and get twenty to thirty wave rides each.

Six hours later, we were heading back from the west side. We saw a wave peel while driving along the coast. No one out. Two to three feet. We surfed for three hours. On the last wave of the session, I got a small barrel.

Pure intention. Visualize. Feel it being already real. Open. Let it become real. Create. You are.

Too much has happened today. Too much distinct and highly impact situations. I need some time for reflection. All I can say for now is what Tim said at the end of our conversation: "If it doesn't work, draw another line."

Waimea is the name of the river that runs into Waimea Bay. It is on the outside of this bay where big waves on Oahu have been breaking for ages. Lately, some men decided to paddle into them and realize whatever they were hoping to achieve.

It has given me more than I could have dreamed of. I guess the biggest gift is the end of doubt. I have no more doubts towards decisions that I make with awareness anymore. In all areas and aspects of my life.

Think about it. On the outside, someone with as little surfing experience as me and being in Hawaii for the first time, shouldn't really take off on waves like that.

A lot of people perceive experience like this to be death provoking. They believe injuries are waiting to happen and traumas related to water and surfing are just behind the bush. They seem quite the opposite to me. Don't get me wrong. I don't surf those waves and focus on falling or getting hurt. Simply put, the ocean always has the upper hand and sometimes we are in the wrong spot at the right time.

On the inside, the Christmas episode and the one to follow on 11th of January, when the waves got even bigger, showed me how deep my understanding of a phenomenon we call "water" has become. I am nowhere near to solving the puzzle. I feel that when humanity does unravel the mystery of 'water', it will find answers to questions about life, energy, structure, information and transformation.

My roommate Matt has played a crucial role in all this Waimea drama. His easy-going approach to start the day enabled us both to be out on Christmas Day at the right time. Since no other spot in our vicinity worked that day, we went for a surf at The Bay. Not because we wanted to prove something, not because we would follow the crowd, not because we wished to conquer anything. Out of shear love for the ocean, surfing and water. Amazingly enough, life somehow noticed that and my wipeout got published in arguably the most known on-line surfing magazine.

In a similar fashion, I returned his 'favour' by talking extensively and in detail about the moments of the wipeout and what I did. Nothing really. Relaxed, that's all. It made him dubious, if he can handle that and it made him contemplate going out on the next day. Still, he did go. He suffered a wipeout on the first wave, which took out one of his contact lenses and bruised his face upon hitting the surface of the water. Calmly, he paddled to the beach, walked to the car, inserted a lens, paddled back to the line-up, caught an even bigger wave, fell even more drastically and came out of all this happy as Larry. He now knows, it is not as bad as it looks if you know how to let go. Amazingly enough, some beings felt how amazing his session was and his photo of a late drop made it onto Surfline too.

Matt Bender, Jernej Rakušček. Florida, Slovenia. Waimea Bay. Photos on Surfline. Roommates. You want more?

My session on 11th went differently, yet it was still transformational. I caught a 'smaller' wave.

The turtle was showing me where to wait for the big one. Yet, I was focusing on the crowd, which was pretty dense, and where to take my line, if I caught a wave, without running over someone. So, I dealt with the people, instead of dealing with the ocean. I paddled for four bigger ones and was sure I would get into them. Obviously, someone was there. Or, someone was taking off deeper than me. I try to refrain from dropping into waves, even at Waimea Bay.

Frustrated enough, I paddled into the beehive and sat with the people. The ocean washed out the frustration pretty soon as that wave came and cleaned half of the lineup. That's why I say it was a 500 dollar's worth of a wave.

In 2006, I spent eight months in Mexico. Mostly surfing Puerto Escondido, known as to be one of the most challenging beach breaks in the world. At least those known to public. My knowledge of riding barrels at that time was so scarce, that I had to pay quite a price, before I would get a four to five meter wave with a tube ride.

It cost around $2000 to repair the boards, so they could get broken again. Twenty times they broke. Almost every week I would take one to the shaper and retrieve a previous one. Some people joked that I bought a new car for the shaper and helped him restore his house. I was heart-broken. Yet, I persisted without asking for any outside help. Boža strongly stood by my crazy side and I am deeply thankful for that.

This time, I decided to address You. I feel my actions have inspired a good number of people. Showed them how anything can be done by a persisting human spirit that has taken the truth based on experiences as a guide. Using the wisdom of the body and ability of mind to train, adapt, observe and eventually play. I intend to give a lot in the future, since an extensive journey into life, energy, surfing and water is finding its way into a book that You now read.

Thanks to anyone who has responded to my Facebook board fund-raising appeal. Thank YOU for being a part of my journey.

INSIGHT

What you realize is what you need to manifest.

Back to Waimea.

It means WAI – water and MEA – red. Red water. Does blood ring an associative bell?

Out of my research, I feel more and more right about my theory that Hawaiian tribes represent a community that has lived by the deepest relation and knowledge of life on Earth. They are as strongly affected by the ocean/water as they are by land/earth. Many of the developed civilizations lack the relationship to the ocean. A real relationship, not just building boats and sailing around.

WAI, WA-ter, VO-da, a-QUA, ag-UA, l'EAU, WA-sser. Please add more.

It seems water carries its own vowel. It makes sense. We ask for water first, then food. We are water on two legs, so it isn't hard to walk on water, if you know what I mean.

Bottom turn is the most important turn in surfing. It connects the whole ride. It is the first turn we do on the wave. If we don't succeed our attempted trick/turn/manoeuvre on the top part of the wave, it is the last turn we do. It defines how much speed we transfer up the wave from going down the face of the wave. Fail or achieve, we always go back to the bottom turn. So in life.

Whether we fall or rise, eventually it passes away. What remains is our "bottom turn". Our core ability to drive from the bottom and go up the face of the wave again. What defines that ability?

It is not a skill. We need to be able. Ups and downs are inevitable. If there is happiness, sadness has to come. Where sadness is, happiness will come in. What stays untouched is our core. It is the essence of who we know we are.

You don't need to know how to describe it. You don't need to get involved into discussions about it. Words. Names. Points of perception. Views.

I have been mostly focusing on my bottom turn in my surfing. It creates space for anything to follow. I know a day will come when I will instantly adapt to the situation, so I'll be to execute what I envisioned.

That quiet, humble knowing on a random day, before you open your eyes to a new day; before your mind starts racing; when you are amazed by the spectacle of a sunset. That is the time your core shines clear to you. A day will come when your core will adapt instantly to any moment of external challenge. Come back. Come back and stay here. In this moment. Welcome.

I spoke to my father on the phone yesterday. We talked about his dad Zdravko, my grandfather.

A son worries about a son. Ironical events of life.

Zdravko is not doing well. My brother took him to the hospital, where he is resting right now. A game of days, they say. I spoke to my mother today. She understood why it is important for me to speak to grandpa. I didn't need to explain. My mother has opened up and started to live the truth. I didn't even notice when the transition happened. It had been there for many years. Eating healthy. Staying hydrated. Doing morning routines. Exploring the nature of her mind. What an exceptional woman.

I felt the sorrow of loss even before I was born. Really. Just after my parents realized that another baby is on the way, my mother's family suffered a fatal car crash. The same day. My mother lost her close family instantly. There was no one they could talk to. No contemplation, no preparation. They said it was a miracle for her not to experience a spontaneous abortion. And so my connection with water began.

Nada, my mother, refused to take antidepressants on behalf of my growing body's development. Thanks for not drugging me straight away.

Still, there was sadness. There was a lot of rain and water on the inside. It felt like in Vancouver, where it either rains or drizzles a lot. I can say it with a light heart now: "Thank you Mother for being sincerely sad and allowing me to connect to the water environment quite early."

They took me to the seaside before I got born. The tradition of spending two or three months in Croatian islands lasted well into my adolescence. Rock diving, swimming, scuba diving, water-skiing, sailing (I was lousy at fishing), and a lot of ball-based water sports. Water, in one way or another, marked my life.

The most influential people I met were either in the water or snow environment. Frozen water in the form of snow significantly affected me until I was sixteen. It was expected that the news of an approaching passing away of my close relative, would come when surfing some big waves.

I only have one grandfather. He is one-of-a-kind. Talk about mind over matter, he could recount his numerous practical applications. Nevertheless, many times people do without knowing what they do and without seeing how to apply it in all areas of life. For, it is a fact – when you learn something, you can apply the knowledge to any aspect. It is called wisdom.

Nada will give me a call when she visits him in the hospital. I hope right words will come my way. I sincerely wish to express the truth about death to him. It is not an end. It is a start. We are here to learn how to come back home in peace. In one piece. Whole. Without fears and screaming. There is no need to cling to anything. There isn't anything. It is just change, a process, a ride.

If you only have one choice, do not only accept it, embrace it. Rejoice in it. It wouldn't be your only choice if it wouldn't be meant for you.

Inspirational it is when someone who is so close to leaving the body, tells you to live to the fullest and have a great time. In - spirit- rational. Holds so many keys.

I spoke to the grandfather tonight. He is accepting his situation. He is at peace. Good. Buddha has taught how the moment of our physical death defines next incarnation; manifestation in "flesh". The state of our mind and awareness. Some claim that it is even possible, if one stays equanimous and calm, to choose how (if) to manifest on planet Earth again.

Grandfather said: "Some people don't believe they would die until the very last minute. But it's a fool's illusion. We are all heading towards death... No sense... Stay where you are and enjoy... I am leaving soon anyway... Just remember the "nagging" grandpa every now and then... I'm fine... The body is weak... I hope it comes soon..."

Now I realize the greatness of his spirit. Now it is shinning through. It has been shining for the last few years, as he started to have medical problems. Obviously, he was fostering cancer in a couple of areas of his body. He would still pass a wisdom or two and share a smile.

I will never know what it took to survive almost

two years of concentration camps, the like of Auschwitz, Dachau and Matthausen. I guess surviving means for us to find a way through the obstacles we set for each other. From one extreme to the other. You were right, Jim Morisson, no one here gets out alive. Viva Life!

Matt is surfing in a surf event at Sunset today. I wish he wins the heats he enters. I wish he comes out with a victory in realization. I'll write about competing in surfing, which is essentially different from other sports, a little bit later. Stay tuned.

I experienced my first bigger injury from hitting the rocky reef bottom today. Actually, I created the opportunity for it to happen. Out of habit. I am trying to refrain from doing it, yet in that moment of safety I reach out to make sure how far out safe I am. Until I go over the line and get hurt.

Shortly after falling with the wave into suspiciously shallow water, I first wait for the impact of the wave to subside. I float as much as possible to stay close to the surface. Then, when the tumbling is about to finish, I, out of no reason known to me rather than stupidity, had (hopefully had, not have) a habit to extend either my leg or an arm to check how close the sharp and rocky bottom might be. Ultimately, I get cut or hurt that way every time.

"I don't know what I'll write about." I said to Val, who came to visit Oahu for some time. "Maybe write about getting hurt on the reef." Spot on.

How many times are we completely safe and then, out of what reason? Why do we go beyond those boundaries only to get hurt? Who is hurting us, if not ourselves by acting towards the situation that hurts us?

Of course, we heal. It is in the nature of nature to support its existential expression. You can keep healing the wounds you keep creating. Or you can let it heal while living a life without hurting yourself.

It seems we need to be super aware to live like that. It is possible, though. I am sure. As Sakae would say: "Guaranteed."

The wave I am about to surf in the next session is already travelling across the ocean.

People's response to my FB appeal, for any donation towards the five hundred dollar board that broke at Waimea, has taken me off guard. Money is trickling into the account. At the same time, a note of my best friend gave me a big mental bone to chew.

He said the money was on the way to Hawaii, but it got redirected towards Haiti in the last minute. Haiti has been hit by a force 7.0 earthquake on January 12. Devastation is enormous. Of course. I will survive with a broken board. Meanwhile, some people need real physical help. This has been the topic of the day.

A dearest friend called me on my cell from her Skype account. She called to get advice. We've known each other for five years now and shared some intense experience of challenge, loss and growth together and separately. I am not able to recall a time when she would honestly, openly ask me for a piece of advice or a word of wisdom. Now, she was completely willing to resolve and finish a pattern that wasn't bringing her peace.

I would keep clear of trying to solve relationship problems of any kind over the email. Talking live via internet video calls would seem as a great idea, but it always left things unresolved. Communicating in person, eye to eye, heart to heart, proved to be the best way, although it would not guarantee success. Above all, minds need to meet. Any resolution in relationships is impossible unless both parties wish to change the current state of affairs. It goes same for helping. Help yourself and help will come.

There is no teaching. There is only learning. We learn from the people who cross our path and, staying true to our experience, they are able to learn from us.

It fails to relate to the case of Haiti in that way. A naturally occurring disaster, affecting lives of thousands of already materialistically fragile society. I know planet Earth is a living being. There is life everywhere on it. Why would it decide to wound places where "weak" society lives? Is it to give "the strong" ones the chance to extend their selfish hand? It puzzles me extensively.

I started training skiing intensively at the age of five and a half. First time I skied, I was four and a half. I have always loved skiing. The competitive focus of a systematical training regimen was something I struggled with. Nevertheless, a keen spirit for learning and a good body coordination were enough to make me a part of the national team for three years, between the ages of twelve and fourteen. In surfing, that would mean to be in the top three to five surfers of the same age plus a year younger or older within such countries as USA or Australia. I slipped a rank under the cut at age fifteen. I had a break from skiing for a year and took up karate in the mean time. My body was too weak to sustain endurable skiing career upon return. The back pain, which was turning into a chronic one and has been there since childhood, was a cherry on the cream or however you put it. I quit competitive skiing for good.

Karate and martial arts legacy engulfed me for the next nine years. I studied oriental texts on developing the unity of mind, body and spirit in order to serve mankind. Protect the weak, if they cannot protect themselves.

Meditating monks were falling asleep during eight to ten hour long meditative sittings. If you wish to have a strong mind, develop a strong body.

"Could you help us, master?" They pleaded.

The master went into the cave and waited for the answer. He came out with a series of body movements, many of which imitated animal gestures. The seed of martial arts.

Who do you compete against in a surf contest?

Is it the surfers in your heat, who have their free will and effect through their minds? Is it the ocean, which you cannot compete with at all? Is it a competition within yourself to stay open and observant amidst pressure associated within your mind? Or are you competing with the system based on rules and judging, hoping to find objectivity in subjectivity?

Plenty of athletes are not familiar with exact rules to which their sport is judged upon. Knowing the system helps you understand what you need to do to be successful. It shows you what is effective and what is a waste of doing. Like the ocean, I can only adapt to them. Find a way to play. Express.

Out of loses, I see the areas of my weaknesses.
Victories show me my strengths.

Ironically, a loss in competition is a more accessible information than a win. On one hand, it shows you where your weak spots are. It is easy to know what could have been done to win. It is a lot more difficult to establish what would have to be done to lose.

How will I compete in a surf contest? Do we really decide who wins or loses, since waves depend on an impersonal phenomenon?

Val and I didn't go surfing today. However, we surfed all day long. We approached the whole day with a surfer's mentality. Observe. Adapt. Go with the flow. Express.

In Haleiwa we met Kim. She explained to me how drinking pure ocean water from depths of a hundred meters improves overall quality of being.

I have been advocating drinking water along with the intake of Himalayan salt, which has 84 to 87 essential minerals for our body. The crystal form corresponds to the membrane settings of our cells, so the minerals can get to where they are meant to go. Inside the cell. The whole vitality resembles the health state of the cells. That's why, cell based diseases, as AIDS, cancer, multiple sclerosis, Alzheimer's and the like, are so fatal. Core beliefs seem difficult to change.

Actually, it is easier to heal than it is professed by so-called healers. Just add water and salt (as a compound of minerals ... forget table salt!).

When drinking it, create thoughts of well-being. Inform the water. Put it into a form. It resonates immediately.

I wish to do the ocean water "therapy". Kim added: "If you drink it in the evening, all the food you've eaten that day turns alkaline." Our body's chemistry is alkaline based. Fact. Acid burns. Fact.

We used hitchhiking as a tool to move around. It showed me clearly what I've been working to improve in my surfing. Now, I see how perfectly it relates to land life.

It was rush hour time. Obviously. There were cars passing the two hitchhiking surfers all the time. A lot of open-tray trucks with a lot of space as well. Somehow, it didn't work. Same thing happened when going to Haleiwa earlier that day. All we needed to do was move from the wrong spot. First time, it was only grabbing our things and stand in the beginning of the bus stop instead in the middle of it. The second time we moved fifty paces.

We surfed on the west side yesterday. The sunset session went down at a small, fast, mostly closing out righthander. There was one small spot to get into the wave in time. Val and I shared a few exchanges and each got a couple of rides. Then, I chose to paddle a little bit further to the right, hoping a bigger wave would let me in earlier and I'd have a longer ride. No chance. And this I've done in many sessions. Believing I would will a wave to break where it didn't. No chance.

Persisting in a rational view of a situation that apparently does not happen is not rational at all. Logically, just move into another space.

Twice we got a ride instantly. Instantly.

Most of the people I've spoken with about big waves have expressed a similar concern. I've spoken to a lot of people about this topic in the last four years. Being what they label as a "big wave surfer", I am fascinated by what concerns them.

It is not a complete loss of control. It is not a risk of injury or even, it happens, drowning. It is not being unfit physically. It is not having the appropriate mindset. None of these, which are essential elements and factors of risk.

It is a fear of not knowing, if they would be able to hold their breath for the amount of time spent under water upon a fall. To hold the breath presents a situation of letting go. The more one is relaxed, the easier it is to stay under water.

When we lose control or when things go the other way as we hoped they would our dependencies come out.

Waves come, pass us by and continue their journey, with or without us riding them. There will always be another movie, a house I can move into, a car that will get me places, a friend who's eye would share a spark. Things come. But, they also go.

This is the wisdom I rely on when I am tumbled around and held underneath the surface by the invisible force (hint: I keep my eyes closed). That's where the strength to stay completely calm comes from. From knowing fully well this fundamental principle of change.

However bad a situation is, it will pass. However strong I wish for good things to come, they are on the way. Enjoy staying in joy.

As I paddle for a wave, I am fully aware of this fact. I know that a wave ride in surfing cannot last forever. It would be nothing but madness though, if I was to pull back just in the moment of catching it. You know. Since it is going to go away anyway, why even bother. Are you in sanity?

This is what we sometimes do on land. We refuse to fully live, because we know how it is all going to end anyway. A relation. A ship. Immerse yourself into it. Love, live, laugh fully. Eternity of the moment.

Death makes you reflect on your past. What you remember you've lived/experienced. Normally, if one sees the past life as being lived to the fullest and without regrets, then one is at peace with the current situation of death. Past defines the present.

Another view of the past, if looked upon with regret and/or remorse, tends to make one feel restless when faced by a warning of the coming death. In reality, you will not know when it will come, when it actually does. Alive. Dead. There is only a moment in between. This moment. It gives me freedom to choose how I view the past, which defines my present, to program (my) the future.

My grandfather passed away from the body today. I dedicated the whole two sessions of surfing Laniakei righthanders to him and his life. On the sunset session I found two barrels and rode them for a while without coming out. A rarity for the day.

I also saw myself in the eyes of my light. As I paddled, I felt a being behind me. A being–of–light. The catalyst. I turned around and, when I felt eyes connect and speak on the informational level of instant moment, I said: "Hi. How are you?" Then the mind read the face. Personalities appeared. We shared a session in Indonesia before. A catalyst. As me. Takes one to know one.

A catalyst is a normal human being. It can have any shape, form and activity motivation. One thing is essential for a catalyst: reflection. A catalyst reflects what is directed towards. Instant karmic creation of reality. What you get is what you give. What you look for is what you see.

Meaning, I can think of my past minutes of a session as joyous ones, thus creating out of a well-being essence in the current moment. This is my reality that creates the future. I change my past and affect the future. With my mind. Time travel. Totally real.

If I am not aware of something, it doesn't mean it is not absolutely real. Example: gravity defined by the tendency of smaller things to be drawn to bigger ones or defined by bigger things pulling smaller ones towards them. To be drawn is to be pulled.

Thank you, Grandpa, for these amazing sessions that we'll keep on having. Welcome to the spiritual world. I could feel you in the ocean today. We were surfing. No problems. I know you saw me too and the catalyst showed me how.

My whole session today was devoted to testing a theory. A practical experiment to experience how true the ancient wisdom of going with the flow of life really is.

Surfers deal with currents most of the time. Actually, all of the time. Even if there is no steady rip current or wind swept water flow, there are currents after a set of waves comes in.

The energy going through the ocean is infinite. Infinitely stronger than a human body. No sense in fighting a battle impossible to win. As in this case. The ocean will not get tired. You will. No point in fighting the current. Most of us and most of the time we do fight it.

The session was great. Even though my 5'10" proved a little bit small for the conditions, I still managed to catch more than ten waves in two hours. In situations where I would usually paddle towards the unbroken part of the wave, I trusted the current taking me towards the oncoming broken wave. I didn't believe my eyes; I followed the feeling of where I was pulled. It worked amazingly well.

Amazingly, because I seem to carry the common seed of the human kind: a belief that there are situations where paddling (moving in life) against the current (chain of events unfolding) makes sense. Like, fighting against the ocean (life) makes sense. We all die though. We all get tired. Ocean stays. Life goes on.

After today's experience I started to doubt any reason to believe in fight and to contemplate a way to use life's flow in any situation.

Where does the tendency to make things hard for us come from? How come we love to complicate things? Why do people strive to burden each other's lives?

Matt argued my view of always going with the direction of the flow. I take arguing in a good way. The power of an argument (reasonable proof) over the argument of power ("I'm right, you are wrong.").

I didn't possess enough wisdom to prove how, what I've experienced, holds the truth. I do know that we are the ones who choose to perform an activity in the environment of the current. We put ourselves there on account of our desires, wishes, choices. It is alright to face the current, but it immediately puts us into accepting to work in order to resist being pulled away from what we've chosen to do, pursue, create, enact, start or finish.

The place we surfed we call "Matt's secret spot". It looks like other people think it's secret too and we were all surprised to meet each other in the line-up. I bet they have a different name for it.

Val expressed her surprise by asking: "Where did all these people come from?"

I replied: "From their mothers." Not to comment her, but to remind myself. We all had or have a mother. We are a lot more similar to each other than different from one another.

On the drive back I explained to Matt how it's been scientifically proven that information surrounding water changes water's vibration pattern through changing the way molecules are organized. A change in the pattern can be photographed and seen if we freeze water and examine its crystal. The purer the water, the more beautifully organized the crystal. They also showed how a word written on a bottle affects the same way. Love and hate both produced what seemed in place.

The original crystal went towards bigger harmony in an ambience of love written on the label of the bottle. Hate transformed it into an even more unorganized mess. Word is a vibration in either sound or sign.

These things have been proven scientifically over and over again. If it all seems far fetched, I simply spill some water over the table full of stuff on it. And observe. I notice how water immediately embraces new environment and adapts instantly. I know my thoughts are powerful. I know from experience that the things I think about actually happen.

When I combine the two types of knowledge, it freaks me out to know that our body is more or less made out of water. Most of our body weight is water. How influential are then my thoughts in this inner ocean of mine? Buddha was right: "There is no idle thought." Every single one gets recorded in the pool of the body. They all get noticed.

Matt said: "If it was that simple, everyone would bless the water they drink."

"Wise men do." Was the reply.

A day of reflection on the circumstances of the injury resulted in this:

Visible, big things encourage us.
Small things hurt us the most.
The invisible thing establishes and takes life.
Let us stay aware.

It has been Val's last day of visit. Of course we got up in the dark. I, again, realized how people miss an amazing hour of each day simply sleeping. We have seen so many sunsets. How many sunrises have you seen?

Seeing and experiencing a sunrise and a sunset in the same day makes me feel I seized it in fullness.

There was no one out at Backdoor or Pipeline. Soon, there were two surfers. Us. Before I went in, I said: "I will get barreled in this session. First wave. Paddle strong. Over the ledge. Oh, there's the tube. I'll pull in. Wow, riding the barrel. Ah, it does not seem to have an exit. I'll just keep riding the tube. Might as well enjoy the view. What?!? A clear exit. Yeah!" The wave let me out and I made it out of a long barrel ride. Magic. Another world. Being surrounded by the ocean water, yet standing on both feet and normally breath air. Magic.

I probably got cocky later in the session. Or something. I'm figuring out the reason for the injury, as I write this. I'll tell you later why it's so important in my opinion to understand the reason behind the injury, "accident", illness or "bad" luck.

I decided to push through the whitewater of a broken wave by guiding the board under it. Not knowing the depth, I changed my decision and tried to jump over. Only tried, being unsuccessful as it was already too tall. Instead of a successful exit, the board turned sideways and came out of the whitewater fast, side rail hitting my upper left thigh. I was, and am, surprised at the accuracy of that hit. Center spot on the spleen point. My whole upper leg went numb a little bit. After almost a day of intensive healing it is still quite sore. At least I can normally walk by now.

The event's details shock me. I didn't get a scratch surfing eight to ten meter waves. But, I get injured on a one and a half meter wave. But, I get injured quite seriously. A kung fu master would hit me like that. Light force, yet completely guided into an acupressure point for the whole muscle, crucial for walking.

How come I didn't feel any sensation of pain while surfing another session four hours later? Even though my leg hurt before and after it, just walking on the beach?

I have my own theory about what is the common reason for people to enjoy surfing. Honesty is a sign of courage, because a person is not afraid to face whichever consequences. Honesty, integrity, fairness. This is what I owe to you. So, here I go:

"My vision of what surfing is and why people, knowing or not, actually devote their time or life to surfing. Others simply do it. Others are amazed by it. Some create excuses. Those, who had the privilege of riding a wave, know the reason. Some vocalize their view. Some live it. Some express it on land through art of any kind.

It seems riding a wave is the primal reason why

we surf. Ironically, 95 percent of our time of a session, or surfing in whole, goes for paddling and waiting. Doesn't matter, we say. We love surfing so much that all the rest (finding waves, travelling, equipment, time management, constant effort, financial cost) is trivial?!?

The wave ride has to possess some kind of a magical power. Surfers act as if they are obsessed. With what then?

Simply by being fully present with an empty mind, because of the way a wave breaks, affects their awareness."

Thank you, Tyler, for a pen and a note five minutes before midnight. I write for this book everyday. No matter what. I ride all the time this wave called a human experience. And it ends eventually. Like my grandfather's ride.

License plate

When saying Aloha, you are basically expressing that you joyfully share (your) life's energy with the person present in that moment.

Determination

We go from no will and all choices
to all will and no choices,
until we decide to create.

Generosity

Whatever is worth having, is worth sharing.

Truthfulness

As it is.

Courage

To be who I am.

Compassion

Whatever I do to you, I do to myself.

Insight

What you realize is what you need to manifest.

Morality

Good and bad are a matter of perspective.

Peacefulness

Through it all, I am back home again.

Loving Kindness

Sailing aboard the ship of relations.

Mexican Pipeline

*Even though the bottom is made of sand,
it is better not to hit it.*

Waimea Bay

The board still had all three fins.
Success.

Merry Christmas

*Neither of us made this one. My board is missing the
right fin and is ten feet six inches long.*

Kaua'i

Napali coast:
the wettest part of the Earth.

Kahuna's advice

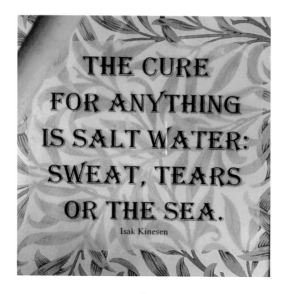

*Ina malama ʻoe
I ke kai, malama
No ke kai ia ʻoe*

Duke Kahanamoku - Aloha ambassador

Until 2010, Duke was the only surfer
to be honored with a statue. Who is now the other one?

MORALITY

Good and bad are a matter of perspective.

They have a ceremony in Hawaii for a respected surfer of the community. They would take the ashes and scatter it into the ocean. Meanwhile, they would wear flower necklaces and sit holding hands, creating a big circle of people, boards, flowers.

We have a funeral. People who didn't say goodbye as they wanted or didn't have a good time with the deceased always suffer the most. I told Zdravko I loved him. I told him I was grateful for all the lessons he had enabled me to have. His death was a passing. Nothing more, nothing less.

There are some members of my family who want me to sit on an airplane and attend the funeral. On one hand, I would love to be there. Especially for my grandmother. It is impossible though. As I said: honesty (to be true to who I am), integrity (to do/say according to my nature/wisdom/knowledge) and fairness (to let you be without judging). This I owe to everyone.

Simon and I had our first session today. As agreed before, I started paying my rent on this planet by teaching and healing. Finally.

Explaining people the truth about death, when they still hold unresolved emotions to the dead one, would not do much good. I am sure. She said it so nicely: "I don't expect anything else of you, but to be happy."

I surfed Pipeline with a couple of world renowned professional surfers today. What do you have if everything you know is only how to surf?

We are human beings on land, nevertheless. Our essence is constantly changing and evolving. Profession is what brings you material wealth and spiritual joy. If it is the only thing you are good at and the only thing you enjoy doing, it will ultimately bring you a lot of misery.

The two wounds connected to "Rocky" and "Backdoor" injuries, along with a sea ulcer that I keep having, appear to be stressful enough for an infection to occur. When it comes to infections, I always ask myself first: "Who are the intruders I let in my life and now have to face and fight?"

Being present is the biggest gift you can get. There's a nice saying about that:

"Yesterday is history, tomorrow is a mystery and today is a gift. That's why it's called the present."

Return to this moment. Return and stay. Stay in the moment. Plan for the future out of real connection with this moment. Reflect on the past to embrace this moment even in a fuller way.

And I've observed and tested it many, many times. It is just the way it is.

Very accomplished surfers never fight the motion of the ocean. A seemingly longer distance to get from point A to point B can be shorter in time if it goes with the current. Straight lines in water are not the quickest way to travel. Good surfers drift in the ocean all session long. They manage their drifting by guiding the board, so that they find themselves in the right place at the right time to manifest a ride. Moving according to the energy travelling through the ocean. There's no general formula. But there is a beat, a pattern for that very day, hour, minute. Some surfers get in tune with it and use it to play. Some fight it.

Some are trying to come up with a formula for a happy life. Some people keep on going against what is happening in their lives. Blind. Seeking.

Lucky few have realized, there is no fixed, end equation/formula/recipe. They follow a general guideline to act from or in accordance with what is as it is. This moment. Adapting. Knowing. Flowing.

Such a marvelous ending of The Peaceful Warrior movie goes like this:

What time is it? – It's now.

Where are you? – Here.

Who are you? – This moment.

If you wish to venture into the moment without the ever-assessing power of mind, drink a big glass of water. While you drink it, focus on the feeling of it going down the throat, the feeling of it filling your mouth, its wetness, its taste. Focus on the sensations of the experience. There you have it.

A sensation can always bring you into the moment. Being aware of any kind of a sensation (no need to name it ☺) is also a way to take away the fuel supply from the "worrying" mind.

Do it whenever you experience losing your composure in any situation. Focus on whatever sensation of the body you can.

WATER

Stars shine
With you they don't
You play with fire
You will get burned
Next to you
No fire burns

Sweetness of air
Is like your presence
Things glow when you are
Around. Abound.

Matt paddled into the unruly ocean at Ali'i beach park, Haleiwa, alone. Marlon and Brian opted to stay on land. Let us observe together.

It looks scary. Although, the conditions are not death defying, the waves are not huge, the currents are not unmanageable. Matt, after successfully surviving the solo mission, reflects upon shark fear. Sitting out there alone made him think about a shark attack.

I suffered a deep psychological trauma with sharks at the age of ten. It took me almost twenty years of mind development, education and real life experience to overcome the phobia of sharks. I was unable to swim in deep water alone. Surfing alone? Forget it. Now, I can do all of those. Oh, what happened in the first place? Classic. I watched Jaws. At a friend's birthday party with the blinds down in a dark living room. I got super-traumatized. Even though I was spending all my summers at the sea and in it, where for a fact no man-eating shark lived, that did not help me one bit, and I was panicky looking around for a fin after seeing a reflection in the water. The reflection was me. As always.

The shark "recovery" proved an ancient wisdom yet again: "Knowledge leads to peace (as in wisdom=knowledge experienced), while ignorance leads to a life in fear."

I educated myself about sharks extensively. I saw a shark, a small one, swim underneath me in Mexico. I could absolutely feel a bigger one close to me on a solo session in Australia. Yeah, right. As if the information travels through water so fast. Of course it does. Don't you think you would feel a bear standing a couple of feet behind you in the forest? Trust your instincts.

There are many factors one can take into account to avoid a shark attack. For example: a lot of fish in the area + no dolphins = some other predator. News of a lot of shark sightings in the area. Outpour of fresh water from rivers after a big rainfall draws them closer to shore. In sharky area, avoid surfing at sunrise or sunset. They are either ending or starting their food hunt. Make sure you see the bottom, because they always circle the prey first. Whatever smell you provide, they will be interested to check it out. And, I love this one; if you see a shark, stay completely calm. It will swim away.

Still, the reality is this:

Almost no one sees a shark coming. The attack happens instantly. The person then just reacts. Please, I am not hoping to get anyone scared here. Quite the opposite. Having experienced deep fears myself, the intention is to shed a light on the subject from a different angle.

Like, when you drive on the road, it's impossible to know where and when a person heading the opposite way will fall asleep, drift into your lane and ... We feel generally safe on the road. If that scenario was to happen, we would instantly react or we might even get a hunch moments prior.

That's my point with sharks. Since there is no way to know exactly, might as well stay relaxed. Staying relaxed gives us a chance to be in touch with our instincts. That is for sure the best way to "know" something is weird. How can you fear the unknown if you haven't got any reference whatsoever about how it would be if it happened? Makes no sense at all.

Many contests occur in one Hawaiian winter at arguably the best wave in the world – Banzai Pipeline. One thing is for certain – you can get the most energized with life tube rides. It's the deadliest spot in the world, since in average a person a year dies here. Two paradoxical ironies in this next paragraph/chapter.

First, the popularity or social expansion of surfing is happening in the most western civilization manner possible through contests, competition and virtual creation of surf stardom, using all kinds of media. For many aspiring surfers get recognized in a competitive format. Bizarre as it may seem, there are contests in surfing. The human mind has yet again succeeded to frame into a system an ephemeral occurrence, in our case surfing.

I met an eleven year young boy from Australia. He is already sponsored by one of the biggest surf industry players. In reality, he has a job. Legal restrictions don't allow him to get paid at the moment, but in a year that will change. From the age of twelve onwards he can start getting paid to surf, for surfing. Real or not, they are supposed to pay him fifty thousand Australian dollars per year.

I paddled out at Pipeline after the first day of Volcom PipelinePro. A valuable event, if you chase those rating competition points. Invaluable, if you wish to catch some of the most amazing waves of your life in a safe environment. We are coming to the second paradox.

There were fifty to sixty surfers in the water. Mostly professionals and locals. The atmosphere was intense. To get a wave it did not suffice for you to read the waves well and know where to position yourself. Not at all. You needed to enter the rat race, dogfight or whatever you name that human behaviour of fighting for an infinite, impersonal resource. That kind of a crowd would be dangerous at any spot, because one had to zigzag between the people while looking for a line on the wave. And what a wave.

Combine that environment with the fact that Pipeline in itself possesses a high risk factor at any size, let alone at the size of that evening with wave face heights of four meters. The bigger the wave gets, the thicker the lip, the more explosive power, yet the depth to a sharp and solid reef remains the same. Adding that to the crowd creates numerous chances for equipment damage, close death calls, injuries and social disruptive actions. Boards do get broken, people do die, fights do occur and I did hold someone's ankle artery to stop the bleeding of the wound on his sole of the feet, sliced open truly deep and well.

The safest way to get the best waves at Pipeline is in a contest. Crazy, is it not?

The competitive nature of our race has created an environment where to be a professional you have to compete against those who are learning to compete. It made me wonder how to get into one of the contests at Pipeline, just so I could peacefully catch a few bombs without putting myself or someone else in a very hazardous situation. There is another way.

I just need to heal my staph infected legs and than put the plan to the test. I still have thirteen days left. The crystal has been charged with strong intention for Pipeline and Backdoor. It never fails to deliver. Water always knows where it flows.

You can save no one,
but Yourself.

In the moment of everyone realizing that, the whole humankind is saved. Saved from what? From feeling separated, scared, ignorant, unhappy.

As a teacher, one has the power to guide and instruct you on the right path for you and you alone. The work has to be done by you. As a healer, one has the knowledge to raise your energy field to a higher state, so you can see the reason. The willingness and openness to the insight is up to you.

The stars have realigned. I changed my plans

accordingly. Now I know why I got hurt at Backdoor that day. To transit from surfing to serving. We are meant to serve each other.

The injury of the thigh interacted with an infection of an open wound that I had on my left knee for two months now. Well, I did not surf for five months prior to coming to Hawaii. The standing up technique was a little bit poor, including the knee being dragged over the pad at the back of the board. A couple of deep reef cuts on the right leg didn't do much good either. I hadn't slept through the whole night for four days. I wake up, because of the throbbing pain in either the left knee or the left thigh.

The body is weak. Mind sharp. Spirit calm. I used the opportunity of healing and meditation to reflect on the whole situation. Everything happens for a reason of our growth to an even bigger well-being. All paths lead to enlightenment. It is our task to embrace and broaden our perspective.

I am glad I waited so long to call Air Canada. I wished to rebook my flights, so I could spend almost a week in Canada helping Dave set up his surf retreat. I also wished to spend a couple of days with Andre in England. The airline helped me by giving no practical options. That engaged me to search for other solutions. Funny enough, is there always a cheaper alternative?

I bought a brand new one-way ticket from Honolulu to Vancouver and it was twenty dollars cheaper than rebooking. I fly out of Hawaii on Thursday, four days from now. The next time I hope to come to Hawaii is in the end of 2011. My dream is to be invited to "the Eddie". But, that's a whole other story.

Some opportunities come to us, we go to realize them,
yet they slip through our fingers, only echoing possible realities.
Not doing something means doing something else instead.
Nothing gets wasted.
The wave always comes.

Year 2003 was a break year of my life. I surfed my first wave before that, but it was that year that I decided to give up the rewards of a successful normal life and headed towards the surfer's dream. I never looked back. And it's getting better each year. Oh, I did lose everything on the way, but the ocean and surfing are giving it all back. Join me on a unique surf journey. You bet, it's a work in progress.

2003. Finished University of sports with honours and was looking at Master's studies of Psychology. Achieved a black belt in Karate. Successfully finished a two and a half year Shiatsu therapist course with a renowned teacher. Made it into the elite ski demonstrator group for alpine skiing to teach ski instructors how to teach. Was in a good relationship with a girl. What did I trade all this in for?

For a one way ticket to the desert and a big plan.

Here's why. Three friends got into a small Ford Fiesta, pilled the surfboards on the roof and headed on land to Morocco for three weeks. Three thousand kilometers just to the border. Of course, Jernej (a.k.a. Journey) had a massive plan to fly out of Morocco, go to Italy, take the train to Slovenia, drive to a small village in the mountain area and attend a one day compulsory pre-season seminar for ski demonstrators. And then rejoin their friends in Portugal. Nothing easier. The one thing that threw that nicely well-budgeted plan out the window was the fact that Jernej somehow forgot his air-ticket in a hotel almost a hundred kilometers away from the airport. Being me, I bought another ticket and flew off to accomplish my plan. Which I did, and I met up with Mare and Simon in Beliche, Portugal, four days after leaving Casablanca.

There on the table everything was ready. Air-ticket, passport and wallet all nicely put in a stack. How I managed to grab everything but the ticket, got me to thinking and lead me to one of the biggest realizations in life: I didn't want to live in the direction I was going!

After the trip, I met with my skiing sponsors, head coaches, university mentors, family, friends, girlfriend and, most importantly, my best friend Mare to explain what's happening next:

We are going on a one way surf trip!

He agreed and off we were.

I remember my last session of a five month long stay in Indonesia in 2008. People ask me where I get the money to travel so much. First of all, I don't travel. I live in different places for a certain time. I am at home wherever I am and at the same time I don't have a home, as people perceive it. Sometimes, it's really hard like that. But it always encourages me to accept the wisdom of who I truly am. A being detached from labelings of this material world.

A human life, if you are aware of it or not, is so fragile. Out of this comes gratitude for each day. Humbleness for what I have, instead of regret for what I don't. My last session was at a spot called G-land. One of the best left reef breaks in the world that can, if a rider and a wave come together just right, give a surfer a ride almost a mile long with plenty of tube sections in between.

We were all waiting for the tide to come up. The waves were good, but the risk of hitting the dry reef so far away from any medical help was enough to keep us all sitting in the shade for a while. After a while, my patience was exhausted. I got ready. Even if I cut myself, it's my last session. I'll heal in Australia. Right? Smart thinking. Anyways, as I started to walk over the exposed reef, a fellow surfer approached me, obviously in shock.

"I think there's a dead body there." He was pointing the finger towards a small, shallow lagoon in the reef and kept backing off in the other direction.

"You are kidding me." I replied. His pale face told me all I needed to know. Death. So natural, still so feared. I was shaking inside, while running towards what seemed to be a body turned face down. I prepared myself, before turning the body around. The eyes penetrate the deepest.

Fortunately, I can be that selfish, his eyes were closed. How heavy a life-less body becomes. I put him down on the dry reef and checked for vital signs. I did many first aid courses and prided myself to be a lifesaver. No signs of life. I started CPR, but the foam coming out of his nose, mouth and ears kept convincing me that it was in vain. Shortly after, his two friends/relatives were beating his chest and crying out loud. There was nothing else for me to do. I faded from the situation.

I collected my board. I saw some amazing tubes breaking over almost dry reef. I was certain of one thing. No matter what situation I'll find myself in that session, I will not jump off the board or hesitate to pull into a barrel. I mean, a young Indonesian boy perished, because he had an epileptic seizure in knee deep water, fell to his knees, lost composure, hyperventilated, inhaled water and drowned while fishing dinner for surfers staying at the camps. No one saw him. No one could help. And I was supposed to be afraid? What a useless way to die.

I will cherish that experience until I die. I got

the best and longest backside barrels that day. I was out alone. No one saw, no one affirmed my success. There's no need for that. You alone know all your victories, you know how much will and effort you put in and all the rest of "proving-to-someone-else" deal. Let your life shine out through your eyes. Your life is amazing. So is anyone else's.

I remember a full moon session. A tiny island next to Fuerteventura, one of the bigger islands in the Canary island group. Los Lobos. A magical place.

Mare and I camped there once for an entire month. Isolation. Probably one of the best times of our lives. Simple, healthy food. Away from the noise. Away from the ego. Just two friends, rabbits, seagulls, mice, rocks, stars, sun, moon, wind, waves, bushes. Surfing the same break on daily basis let's you see it in a different way. You become a friend. You get to know the rocks, how they sit together, how they form shapes in the bottom. You get to see how wave energy bends around them, how it twists, breaks and pushes. Naturally then, when the sun hits the moon so brightly, away from light pollution, and its silver reflection dances on the surface of the sea, and you know the daytime version, and there is no one surfing, you wish to go out. It may seem scary, but you know the spot.

We woke up slightly before 2 am. You would be able to read a book. Or see your hand's lines in the moonlight completely. No flashlight needed for the walk. We knew the rocks and found our way into the lineup safely. The reflection of the light from the moon was so bright that it actually blinded us when trying to see the coming sets. But, we know the spot, we argued. We trusted our argument.

I don't even remember who caught that wave first. What's important is that there they were. Two Slovenians sharing a ride with the full moon. Drawing lines around each other, so we didn't collide. Turn after turn for over fifty meters. What a ride! Not only were the outside settings "to cry out with joy" beautiful, the inside revelations matched that intensity.

We ride the wave in order to express ourselves fully in the moment. No social cover-ups, no personal make-ups. No time for that. You are who you are when you ride a wave. It makes sense how some get annoyed when others come onto the same wave. It takes away full freedom to express the way one would wish to. For, where I'd draw a line, there is someone and I am frustrated.

Yep, frustration grows if you keep focusing on the obstacle. That can get you really pissed-off. Still, better to be pissed-off than to be pissed-on. And we usually piss against the wind.

It is rare to share a ride with someone. You might get to surf your whole life with a beloved friend, but how many waves have you shared? I believe it is a practice of spontaneous communication to ride together. We both have to adapt to the wave, yet keep expressing without hindering each other's freedom to. Truly an art of living. Now, I am not encouraging you to drop into waves with everyone or invite people to join you for a ride every time. It's not safe to practice extremes. Yes, life is deadly and we all die, but there is no need to be or to get hurt in between.

I do encourage you to share some waves, when safe to do so, and find your freedom to express your inner being in the moment with joy and harmony with other beings. Aloha.

Tim is taking one of my boards to Australia for me. Don is taking care of the magical board. Yuto bought the 8'0" that I needed to sell. Dave is picking me up at the airport tomorrow. Andre is looking forward to my visit in England. Roberto is happy with the work we've done. The list goes on and on. We are angels of realization to each other. I like that.

Let's talk about how surfing reflects life. A human experience in life, that is.

When we enter the ocean, we leave the past on the beach and find ourselves captivated by the present. The future is left uncertain. We are the masters of our destiny. We decide where, when, how and with what board we paddle into the ocean. Control it we cannot. Our power lies in observation, adaptation and using the energy at play for our amusement.

We have our board. That resembles the legacy of our ancestors on land. It is a result of the past trials and errors. An evolution in knowledge.

We use our two small hands to move in a space as vast as the ocean. Similarly on land, we use our feet (or wheels) to move from here to there. The highest influence on how we will experience a session is our will to keep paddling. When (if) the will is gone, the pursuit becomes meaningless. We look for the shortest, easiest way to get back onto the safe land. We look to return to our comfort zone. To where we think we have control.

We may choose the wrong board according to our knowledge. Or conditions. We might use the wrong approach to overcome a challenge on land. Or we are not able to meet the demands of the test. Better not to go into the ocean until we have the board (knowledge) and/or we are confident in our paddling (skills) to face the ocean's pulse.

Some people just use the same board regardless of the conditions. They look to apply it adaptively. Some people are just afraid to experiment and learn something new. They might fall on a wave and end a ride. Well, every ride finishes. So?

Some people turn into excuse-artists, creating illusional realities for them to excuse themselves from surfing. Some simply know the waves won't stop and attend momentary issues on land. For as long as the sun shines, swells will happen. And for as long as there is water, the energy will travel through it.

You find that spot where a wave might break. You go to 'university' where you might learn valuables. You sit, observe, study and wait. For the test to come. And it always comes. Sometimes you are ready, sometimes you are not. You paddle to catch a wave. You pick up the pen and start answering the test. You get to your feet, and give the test to the teacher. You ride the wave. You end the ride. Happy for the experience. Humbled by the connectivity of it all. You passed the exam and exit the 'university'. You are back on land and you implement what helped you succeed at surfing into life situations on land. Somehow, the knowledge from university, if applied correctly, seems to improve more than just the financial side of your life.

PEACEFULNESS

Through it all, I am back home again.

Here I am again. Same airport, completely different man. The biggest, funniest paradox of it all: "the only constant is the change, yet one thing remains the same and it cannot be given a name". Two and a half months ago since Jernej landed at Honolulu airport. The nose surgery that activated the other half of the brain. The rides of thirty feet waves. The visit of a being-of-light for two weeks. The heart's resolution. The death of his grandfather. The fund raising party. The relationship with turtles. The people he met. Who is it now that writes these lines?

It's Jernej, but a completely different one. I am no longer the man who doubts. Breath of life (Ha). Water of life (Wai). Its essence and power. A place for the gods (self-realized human beings of light and awareness). Amen. Come and be open to Hawai'i. Time is not important. Only love is.

Whatever awaits me in Canada with Dave, in England with Andre and Dominiq, in Canary Islands with Mare, in Australia with Caron, wherever with whomever is going to be the result of this moment. Present creates future and past. For it is good now, my future is good too. Ways of manifestation are unknown, free of potential possibility. The core is what I determine now. Good things lead to good ones. What goes around, comes around. What I give, I receive. Instantly.

You realize now why loving yourself first is of the utmost importance? Love lives on the inside. It is the secret ingredient, defines intention. Outside action manifestation is a vehicle of love. A kiss can hurt. A slap can help. The intention determines karma, re-act-ion. Re-in-acting.

I saw a master chiropractor two days ago. Thank you Matt for taking me along. Tom readjusted spot on what needed to be done. The health of the spine truly outlines overall health. We are electricated water vehicles. Tssss. One would assume surfers, with their chests bulging out and behinds butting up, have healthy postures. Not really. The key to having a good posture is by having strong core muscles, those located in the abdomen area below the navel. Six-packs look nice, but they are not functional without strong lower abdomen and back muscles. They keep the pelvis bone in the right position. This enables the shoulders to relax, the head to go into correct place and the relaxation of neck muscles follows. I mean, your neck is where your head connects to the rest of the body. Life is much more than living inside your head with thought preoccupation.

Surfing connects you with the whole of your body, from toes to the hair-ends. It washes worries away.

Even if you don't catch a wave. How about that for a disclaimer?

"I guarantee You that surfing will make You feel better, make You feel again at all, make You relaxed, open, fill You with moments of joy, presence, even if You don't experience the essence of surfing, as in a wave ride."

Sounds like a waterproof business plan! Bullets make no sense, since water penetrates and melts everything in time.

And it is. Surf schools, surf camps, surf retreats, surf associations, surf oriented businesses, surf "you-name-it"'s are springing up around this blue planet as mushrooms after the rain. Maybe it is the age of Aquarius, maybe it is getting hot, maybe it is a low start-up cost, maybe it is the power of offering fun even when instructors are under qualified. Maybe. I don't know.

What I do know and have seen happening around the world is that I don't really have to be a good surf teacher/coach/instructor for people to have fun in my lessons. Surfing is the easiest way to "sell fog". People come, have fun, pay and go. How many take up surfing for real? Not a lot.

As someone who represents the first link between new clients and the wisdom of surfing, it is my responsibility and obligation to show them how amazing surfing is. More. To teach them ways of movement that will not hinder their progress in the future. I am not here to judge who will get the 'surf-bug' and who won't. I am here to treat them all with respect and honour their time and energy in money form, which they share with me.

True teacher never stops learning.
Teaching is the best way to learn.

By following these guidelines, embracing water's properties, studying current board design, referring to how the body learns new movements, implementing how the mind affects learning, I devoted ten years to create an open, yet systematically organized method to teach and learn surfing. This is the purpose behind my visit in Vancouver in six hours.

There is never enough time to do everything I could do. There is always enough time for what I do do. I said to Matt when leaving: "Always joking, but dead serious." Oh, yeah, and it is possible to ultimately know in advance.

All my stuff, along with all the gifts, fit into the surfboard bag and the travel bag. Just fine, so I could close the zips without a struggle. I was allowed two pieces of luggage, each weighting fifty pounds (23 kg). The weighting scale at the airport showed: surfboard bag = 53 pound, travel bag = 51 pounds. Not exactly fifty, but come on! Get serious.

Great achievements go to those who follow great dreams. Doing something differently than you normally do can only create a gain in knowledge, whether you succeed or not. It is impossible to learn without mistakes. In the end, you can always go back to doing things the way you usually do them. You do it anyway. Aspire. Inspire.

Day one with Dave in Canada rated as success. In fullness. Teaching and learning by teaching it, the wisdom of water as a medium for the energy pool to express itself in such momentousness that what will stay unnamed is giving me rejoice you.

All the time in life we are moving forward. We don't walk backwards. We don't drive backwards. We surf forward. We are going through life by moving forward through it. No one is forcing us to move. The essence of life is to move forward and to change. That is what we are. Life. Impossible to lose, what you don't have. We don't have life, we are life.

We move through itself walking on water, that which constitute our body and resembles light. Riding it, as if it would be a wave. It is. A wave of energy, of a dance and play of our self-knowing being.

Surfing is riding the waves of energy and embracing the gift of presence to the present moment in life. What time is it? Now. Where are you? Here. Who are you?

In the hostel, where Dave and I are staying for the second night in adorable Tofino on a, shall we say green, Vancouver Island, I shared a supper discussion on the health care system, insurance and banking. The usual. Foremost, I am deeply grateful for the lecture on those topics by a charismatic, vital lady of something's, who had worked as an expert in those fields for decades. I wish to thank Dave B. for being such a pure reflection of the Self.

The conversation showed and approved that which I felt was right for me to strongly advocate for a while now: "Investing money in your well-being; that is food, exercise, books, holistic treatments, travel, education; instead of paying it to someone else on the basis of incapability to be responsible for your happiness, will always be a more economical solution. And a more enjoyable one."

Months later, as I am reviewing this text, I feel I need to add what has been confessed to me recently by an executive of an international pharmaceutical company. She told me how feelings and sensations we have get labelled as symptoms of diseases without any proof whatsoever. In other words, they come up with a new list of so-called symptoms. Why? Are you really asking that question? To sell more and newer chemically made, body destroying products we don't need, is the answer.

As I passed on the gift, he said: "Great. We have money. We'll pay you. How much do you want?"

"You don't have all the money you don't need to give me."

How come we possess the power to understand paradoxes? Only a view that has seen both sides really grasps the whole experience. Maybe. One thing is for certain. Matt Bender has to be catching some crazy waves soon. First night in Vancouver, a song echoed through the apartment building. It kept playing in Matt's car – "Sweet Home Alabama" by you know who. Go Matt, go!

The weekend with Dave finished. Audrey welcomed us with a delicious dinner. What a closure of an experiment in time. We totally expanded it with being present and it feels we've been away for a week. We covered a lot. Time to rest now and put it all in writing in the days to come.

The surf in Tofino over the weekend was refreshing. It's been amazing to see how different an experience in different locations can be, yet it holds the same essence. Riding waves is equally enjoyable anywhere in the world. How we get to them and the environment they break in varies significantly. Surfing in cold water takes you out of the comfort zone of the habituated mind, brings you back and leaves a very refreshing feeling on your skin afterwards. Actually it didn't really feel as cold as I expected it to be. Now, that's a funny statement, don't you think?

If you had five days of your life left, how would you pass on what you've learned? Do you know how much time you've got left? Start sharing your knowledge. Everyone has a story to tell.

You are not able to foresee your whole future. You are able to see the present clearly enough to keep walking on the right path.

Here I am. Vancouver airport heading to England. Writing into a notebook that was bought for an entirely other purpose three months ago. Remembering how I felt, gave me the will to help whenever, however I can. Sometimes a smile makes someone's day. Most of the time, actually.

Dave and I had a farewell dinner at the Belagio last night. A beautifully intriguing Portuguese woman named Myra served us. She, as many others in these past years, resonated to the simple fact of me writing a book. I felt she was a lot more spiritually evolved than it appeared to the eye. We talked. She exposed something, which is really the core of why we keep lingering in confusion: "So easy in theory," she said "but so difficult to put it into practice."

Why? It puzzles me. Practice seems so much fun.

I enjoy long flights. What other way to have all the time in the world to reflect on life on land? The perspective is also quite good. What we call a problem looks mighty small from thirty thousand feet. We put ourselves smack into the middle of them, so they become enormous. Then we either get angry, complain or get confused.

Upon arriving to London Paddington train station, I asked the train officer where to catch the train to Newton Abbott. He pointed out the place, but also informed me that there was a fatality and the trains are suspended until further notice. The calmness in his voice, when he expressed the word 'fatality', shocked me. Being on a mission to find tickets disabled me to contemplate what he meant. I saw a lot of people waiting. Then, the announcement came. The race began. Would I consider moving through the stampeding crowd going the other direction, it would be a waste of time. Just standing in a little corner proved to be in people's way. Everyone concerned only about themselves and still they wonder, how come no one cares for them.

By staying in the flow, I got the tickets in time and got on the 14:06 train. I arrived at the station from Heathrow at 13:50. The sandwich I ordered and ate was enjoyed in peace and an ambient of knowledge that I am open and connected.

"Three trains in one." The manager explained why many of us cramped the walkways. Put first class citizens in a third world situation. They get angry or complain. Do the reverse, they get greedy and confused. Somehow, I can't see us having a worse day than the soul who threw its body against the windshield of the on-coming train. Death has a big impact on life.

Before I got to the passport control, I saw a big

poster for an international management company that pictured an elephant riding a surfboard. Really. Accenture.com. It seems I am exactly where I am called to be. Again and again.

So are you. But you wish that life conformed to your view, instead of seeing what you can realize in the current situation. Everything, all the time, is for a reason of return to happiness.

"Andre, your wetsuit's hood is in the dog pee!" Claire shouted. Classic. Dogs. Welcome to yet another home away from home. They say 'home is where your heart is'. Well, my heart is right here all the time.

Catching a wave. In the beginning, I have no idea of how to relate to the visual information of a travelling wave. With my paddling I am searching for that entry point. For that moment, when it slows down a bit, rises up a bit and starts to tip over. Remember, we actually surf a breaking wave in front of the breaking point. Those lucky enough, surf behind that point, inside the wave.

Now, if I wish to catch a wave, I need to paddle with it and get to my feet at the right time to go down the face of it, do the bottom turn and start realizing the ride. I need to wait for the impulse of speed, not the impulse of lift or push. Speed. When the board starts gliding faster than I am paddling, the entry point appears.

When we catch up with the speed of the events unfolding in our life, we can stop exerting and flow with them. Standing up, of course.

Usually, I need to go through a trail and error like process, if I wish to learn evaluating the breaking wave efficiently. Many times people tend to gravitate to one extreme end of their experience. For example, the wave passing under them, while they get to their feet without any change in speed. Something lifts them up, they get scared of the drop and look for safety in holding the rails, while trying to get to their feet. Others paddle hard, fully focused, intended to succeed, but they forget to focus on the wave as well, so when they find themselves travelling faster, it's already too late and they fall face forward or, as we say, go over the falls.

Compare these two extremes to everyday life.

In order to find the dynamical balance one needs to experience both ends of the extreme. If I keep getting projected forward from the top of the wave, then I could move further out to sea and attempt from the other end. Or, if the wave keeps passing me under, then I need to breathe deeply and move closer to shore, closer into the breaking action of the wave. No sense in persisting in one extreme. Eventually it gets tiring, frustrating, conflicting.

Similarly, when I explain to people that they are chronically (i.e. lasting effect in time) dehydrated, I see how they embrace the wisdom, start drinking more good water, start consuming the right type of salt, I notice a mixed feeling of excitement and doubt.

Excitement comes from knowing that when more people get in touch with water inside, more people will begin the process of awakening. And we really could wake up finally.

Doubt, on the other hand, arises from observing that they stay in that one end of the extreme, the dehydrated one. Yes, I know now, and I drink more water with adding some salt now and then. But, you were living extensively, for years, decades, being dehydrated. If you are attempting to establish a normal level of hydration in your body, mind, thus spirit, then you need to keep chronically hydrating yourself.

Have water at hand everywhere you go. Start the day with water. End it with it. Have it by your bed. At the reach of your hand in the work place Take sips all day long. Let food get digested straight after the meal without it. Compensate with it – your body loses four parts of water for every part of coffee. Eat food that is not salted with processed salt. Enjoy fruits. Use vegetables. Avoid refined sugars. Let water flow into your life fully. Embrace its wisdom. While you drink it, bless it with whatever a positive intention you find creative. Talk to your plants. Treat your pets. Communicate with your body. They are all more or less water in a form, informed water on legs.

Water reacts instantly. Reflects the vibration and intent of the environment immediately, clearly. Get it? I wish you got it.

I'm waiting for Andre. He is consulting the surgeon who will operate his spine next week. There are a lot of people in the waiting room. As popular as hospitals may be, you don't wish to visit one or stay here. There is a much more simple, cheaper, efficient way to go. Flow.

People make mental constructs to build and support sensual addiction.

"I'm waiting for the blood stats to go up," he said to someone over the phone.

I went along with Andre to visit his good friend who has been undergoing chemotherapy. He has been diagnosed with leukaemia. A malfunction on the level of blood cells. Cancer is a cellular disorder. Yet, it has been proven that we all possess cancerous, damaged, irregular cells. Likewise, we house beneficial and harmful bacteria. Keeping it all in balance, that's the key. The inside of someone who is diagnosed with cancer cells that are taking to start over is at war. And 'the bad guys' are winning. Time to create a place of peace. Disarm with love.

But, people love problems. Love to keep away from being responsible for their health.

"Waiting" I thought. "What do you mean, you are waiting? For what?!? The chemotherapy kills everything." The good and the bad. I, for sure, wouldn't just sit and wait. And drink coffee (one of the most toxically treated plants on the planet) with white sugar and milk from cows treated with too much to mention. And eat gum-candy with pork gelatine.

The funny thing is that the poor fellow does not even know anything is wrong. The doctors are curing me. I am taking super strong vitamins. I'm on the up. I might get affected real quick. Maybe we could smoke a joint?

At war. Stressing realistic contradictions of one's Self.

How many people got cured of cancer/AIDS with following the western medicine approach without a change in their lifestyle? In mathematics, it's not a number. Interestingly, it is impossible to determine which was the most influential factor of those causing cancer. Smoking? Eating processed food? Dehydration? Stress? Mental habits? All of the above?

Easy to get lost and give up. J. Morrison wrote it perfectly: "No one here gets out alive." That's exactly why we have all the right to enjoy it to the fullest. Enjoyment and pleasure, sorry, are not the same.

The most mistake-proof approach I could adopt is to change everything! What I eat, how I behave, mental habits, exercise, everything! This way, if I still die to the illness, my quality of being in the last days may be the highest possible. But, and this is likely to happen, if I overcome disharmony, achieve peace, heal, then I transformed a curse into a blessing.

There are no curses, only courses.
The lessons wrapped-in blessings.
The task is to find the real cure.
To heal is to reverse the effect.
Now rest. Meditate on that.

Saying it is useless to help people who do not wish to help themselves, thus be helped in the first place, is only partially true. I have no power to heal you if you don't wish to heal yourself. Why on earth would I waist the effort of healing you, if you truly did not wish to be healed? More fighting will not help at all.

Intellectually, maybe that's fine. Energetically, there is a natural inclination to help someone in need. Where the lock is, the key exists. The very need to help someone in need is the reason why we developed such complicated, partial approaches to healing. We are being taught to find a solution to the problem created specifically for creating the need for that solution.

LOVING KINDNESS

Sailing aboard the ship of relations.

Google search. Water. Click. Wikipedia. Click. Water is the most abundant substance on Earth. It is in a dynamical equilibrium, always circling from one form into the other. Let it go. Let it come.

Gizmo. Topper. Andre. Jernej. In an astonishing English landscape, the mind grew silent, the breath calmed down, and the sounds of nature started to fill the domain of senses. The easiest way to see through anything is a walk in the nature.

It is also a chance to see the expanding nature of time in as simple of a symbol as a tree. It grows from a single seed. It grows slowly, persistently, silently. To reach the outer layer beyond which the sun's rays become abundant. Expanding, spreading wider. Look at a leafy, leafless though, tree. See its network of branches. How they come out of one trunk, out of one line of explosion. Now, freeze. Freeze in time, what you are observing. Do you see now, how a tree is an explosion of a seed, if you fast forward in time?

Complicated as it might be, the tree and the river may as well be the best natural teachers of life. With a big mind trip to experience them that way! Right.

Putting things in perspective is great, but in the end, we face reality from our usual point of view. Could it be that a single place exists, where we experience the same regardless of our previous moments and/or any filter we might carry?

Example: when flying across the ocean, people get put in a small area, where they find their own way to deal with circumstances of an airplane flight. The same situation, x number of experience. It goes like this for every case. We live the same life, yet we experience it differently. This is the gathering place: living it. In surfing, people meet in that moment. We surf, because of power. The ocean is always changing in the present.

As contradictory and confrontational our ways of how we choose to live as they may be, they are but expressions of the same attempt: to live in the eternal moment of joy. Change is forever, joy is for now.

Two waters meet, join their course, share their energies and play in abundance. Partnerships get born and flow down the stream of life, towards the ocean of eternity. Very poetic. Maybe it's valentine's day's vibes ...

Among many other insights, a nice slogan came flying in: "B smart = Body Spirit Mind ART". Enjoy the walk.

Courage for the body.
Truth for the mind.
Wisdom for the spirit.

Let us go for a ride, travel to London, fly to Fuerteventura and return to where it all started, where it will stay.

Marko is leaving for Slovenia for a week the same day I fly to Fuerteventura with the same plane I am flying in. What a curious sequence of events. It all happens simultaneously. First time we came to Fuerteventura was seven years ago.

"It's simply too cold." Marko commented the freezing temperatures already lasting for a week. We had a trip planed to Morocco, but it seemed so far away. The price of a return ticket showed us what needed to be done. Two weeks after, we were back. We had found our winter paradise. Same year, almost ten months later, I had the chance to enroll into a master's course for psychology; I had a steady relationship with a great girl; I made it into the skiing's teaching elite. It all came together. A simple plan. Study semesters, instruct future ski teachers, save up money and surf for four months full on.

Well, what can I say to explain why I had a one-way ticket, a couple hundred Euros, an open heart and a trusting mind, just before it all took off? I am certain of one thing. Going camping in the desert north territory of Fuerteventura with Marko, becoming broke in the process, living in a tent away from civilization for three months, getting work through some "angels", and realizing that it's possible to have a lifestyle I dreamt of, were one of the best decisions I had ever made.

Looking back now, taking in also seven years that

followed, I can understand what a magical journey it has been. Surfing made me perceptive to how the energy travels, how it reshapes around forms of obstacles, how it affects water, how to live life on land. I feel my life is completely in my hands and it's the best feeling – feeling of freedom to express unlimited joy in a limited way.

Limited, because every single decision shapes the reality of experience and opens an array of future endless possibilities. The more we keep an imaginative mind, the more different possibilities we see. Thus, it is unlimited as well.

Is surfing so important to me?

A lot of energy and time goes for it. If I hadn't learnt what I had learnt, I wouldn't have felt humbled by experiencing it. Through transcending its rules, values, laws and points of view, I began to surf life on land. Day by day. Session by session.

We in the end, as surfers, return to land eventually and by land we are supported. Re-source.

Now. It's time to share.

Breathing air. Standing. Surrounded completely by water. There is always light at the end of the barrel. Your answer has been questioned.

Thanks for reading. Until next time, and always, Aloha.

END = START

Acknowledgements

Photos (in order of appearance)

- Cover - A. Rigler: Sunset from Fuerteventura's beach; Wing - J. Adamič: Author's portrait
- A. Frenda: Sketch of the mandala (sketched by Spike)
- J. Rakušček: Hawaiian license plate
- Determination - A. Frenda: Determined plants on Los Lobos island, Canary islands
- Generosity - A. Rigler: Sunflower
- Truthfulness - J. Rakušček: Rainbow tree on M'aui, Hawai'i
- Courage - (unknown): Portrait in front of Banzai Pipeline, O'ahu, Hawai'i
- Compassion - J. Rakušček: The dry earth on Los Lobos island, Canary islands
- Insight - J. Rakušček: One of many astonishing sunsets in South Australia
- Morality - J. Rakušček: The green and wet part of Victoria, Australia
- Peacefulness - B. Majstorovič: Sunset at the monoliths, South Australia
- Loving kindness - A. Frenda: Different plants living side by side on Los Lobos island

- R. Piña: Beach break at Puerto Escondido, Oaxaca, Mexico
- D. Palama: First ten meter wave of my life at Waimea Bay
- T. Reis: The Christmas gift by Pacific Ocean at Waimea Bay
- J. Rakušček: North coast of Kaua'i, Hawai'i
- J. Rakušček: A nice thought inside Paradise Cafe, Hale'iwa, O'ahu
- J. Rakušček: The statue of Duke Kahanamoku at Waikiki Beach, Honolulu

I am deeply grateful to my parents. My father, Borut Rakušček, enabled me to embrace physical training and my mother, Nada Žemva, connected me to the water element. My grandfather, Zdravko Rakušček, has shown me the resilience of the human spirit and my grandmother, Felicita Rakušček, the vastness of a loving heart.

Marko Mrzlikar has come along on the first real surfing trip and has shared this self-taught journey into surfing with me to this moment. Luka Krajnc has seen and always supported my inner light. Matej Kandare has shared his passion for travelling and skiing. He has been one of my closest friends for decades. Jure Gostiša and Jernej Podlipnik had gone through a lot of crazy adventures with me and had given me courage in respecting the path I have chosen. Boža Majstorovič had supported me, in one way or another, through the venturing years around the globe. Ariane Frenda, Roslyn Dekker, Caron Miller and Val Lynne Frey had been angels for my heart. Katja Špur has enabled me to stop in my restless steps and start the process of settling down on this earth. My sincerest gratitude to you all.

A group of friends: J. Stipanič, D. Aleš, I. Plevnjak, N. Brkovič, I. Troha, T. Kokalj, B. Sinčič, A. Glavan; were the right people in the right moment at the right time to give me space for some of the most important insights of my life. A big "hookey" to you all!

There are numerous other beings met along the journey who had shaped me into this moment. I wish them all the best and may we meet again one day to share stories.

Urša Selan Kovačič and her husband Viki made a great job of going through this text of flow. They contributed to some parts with their remarks and helped me to organize the book into chapters. Thank you.

The author of the foreword, Don, has graced me with coming into my life and showing me how to embody the essence of aloha spirit. Thank you. The magic board is waiting. Mahalo.

Session notes

Session notes

Session notes

Session notes